Do I Need to See the Doctor?

A guide for treating common minor ailments at home

FOR ALL AGES

DR. BRIAN MURAT and DR. GREG STEWART

WILEY

John Wiley & Sons Canada, Ltd.

This edition published in Canada in 2004 by
John Wiley & Sons Canada, Ltd.

Library and Archives Canada Cataloguing in Publication

Murat, Brian, 1960-
Do I need to see the doctor? : a guide for treating common minor ailments at home / Brian Murat and Greg Stewart. — Nova Scotia ed.

Includes index.
ISBN 0-470-83650-4

1. Self-care, Health. I. Stewart, Greg, 1960- II. Title.

RC81.M87 2004a   616.02'4   C2004-906850-4

1 2 3 4 5 FP 08 07 06 05 04

Cartoons by Chuck Temple
Conceptualized by Drs. Murat and Stewart
Production Coordination by Tim Withey
Graphic Design by Ron Sumners, Sumners Graphics
Printed by FP

Macmillan Canada, an imprint of John Wiley & Sons Canada, Ltd.
6045 Freemont Boulevard
Mississauga, Ontario L5R 4J3
www.wiley.ca

Attention

The approach to medical problems is always in evolution. The incorporation of new research, broader clinical knowledge, new technology and new medication may change the best way to manage medical problems. The writers, editors and publishers of this book have made their best effort to create a publication which uses the most up-to-date information available and have given advice that, at the time of publication, would be in accord with standards of practice. However, in view of human error, changes in medical science or misunderstanding by the reader, neither the writers, publishers nor any other party involved in the preparation or distribution of this publication warrants that information contained herein is in every respect accurate or complete, and they are not responsible for any errors or omissions or for the results obtained from use or misuse of such information. Readers are to be aware that this publication does not at any time replace medical practitioners and that people should always seek out a medical opinion if they feel it is warranted.

Registered Trade names used in this book are identified by bold print.

Printed in Canada

To our mothers Helen and Donna

Whose practice of commonsense home-based therapy is an inspiration. They swear that we are alive today as a direct result of their therapeutic application of a tincture of time, a mustard poultice, or a gravol suppository whenever they were needed.

Acknowledgements

We would like to express our sincere thanks to the following individuals whose assistance in creating this book was invaluable.

Dr. John Rea
Dr. Dann Morton
Dr. David Mathies
Dr. D. A. Jarvis
Dr. Derek Jones
Dr. Wendy Alexander
Dr. Su Sundaram
Victoria Mathies
Jane Withey
David Chilton
Bill Coon
Mary Jane Gordon
Heather Scott
Donna Lynch
Dr. Peter White
Walter Tedman

The following Registered Trademarks are used in this publication and are identified within using bold print.

Advil
All Bran
Allegra
Aspirin
Auralgan
Axid
Bactine
Benadryl
Biaxin
Bran Buds
Burosol
Chloraseptic
Chlor-tripolon
Claritin
Colace
Correctol
Dimetane
Dimetapp
Exlax
Fleet
Gastrolyte
Gaviscon
Gravol
Hismanal
Imodium
Kaopectate
Kool-Aid
Lansoyl
Maalox
Metamucil
Milk of Magnesia
Motrin
Pedialyte
Pepcid
Peptobismol
Polysporin
Prepulsid
Prodiem
Riopan
Rolaids
Sennakot
Solarcaine
Surfak
Tagament
Tavist
Telfa
Tums
Tylenol
Vasocon
Visine
Wild Strawberry
Zantac

The recommendation by the authors to use specifically named products in this publication is based solely on the authors' practice patterns. The list in no way represents the entire range of products available, nor does it suggest superiority over other products on the market. The authors recommend that consumers ask their pharmacists for advice about product purchases.

Table of contents

When children are sick with:

When adults are sick with:

Other illnesses or symptoms

Information pages

FOREWORD

When Brian and Greg asked me to write the foreword to this book I leapt at the opportunity. "Do I Need To See The Doctor?" belongs in every household in Canada. Unlike most of the other self-help medical books with which I've become acquainted, it's neither too big nor is it intimidating. Certainly, none is as instructional as "Do I Need To See The Doctor?" This book is designed to help the reader develop the confidence and skills necessary to care for common illnesses at home. If you've ever awoken at 3:00 in the morning to the sound of a child coughing uncontrollably or experienced the helplessness of a parent trying to deal with a child suffering from earache, this book will be a welcome addition to your home. Its beauty lies in its simplicity. It will empower you to become a more capable decision-maker resulting in an educated consumer providing good healthcare in the home.

In my professional capacity as Chairman of one of Canada's fastest growing benefits and workplace wellness consulting firms and as the Chairman of the Wellness Councils of Canada, I am all too familiar with the heavy toll that excessive and unnecessary visits to the physician can place on the cost of healthcare in this country. Never was this phenomenon more apparent than during my tenure as Chairman of the Board of my community hospital. I am extremely excited about this book and its potential to serve as a catalyst for meaningful and beneficial change.

The fact that the use of this book will result in fewer medical visits, less testing and less antibiotic use in self-limiting illnesses is secondary to the fact that it is simply promoting good medicine. The book will improve the skills of the average person to safely and confidently care for themselves and others yet know when they should consider accessing the medical system. These are the skills that people are looking to develop. "Do I Need To See The Doctor?" is designed to develop in people the skills that they do not have. Look at the book as it is today. Pick it up again as you'll undoubtedly do a year or two from now, and you'll be pleasantly surprised at how it has become dog eared and well worn. Like a comfortable pair of slippers, this is a book to be used, not hidden away in the dark recesses of some closet.

Ed Buffett
Chairman, Wellness Councils of Canada

The Family Medicine Chest

Illness and accidents don't happen on a schedule. Have you noticed how often children get sick at night? We advise you to plan ahead and avoid delay. We suggest that you have the following products in your home for quick treatment without delay.

Acetaminophen (**Tylenol**, **Tempra** or generic)
in liquid, chewable tablets or regular tablet form as appropriate for age. Check the dosage chart on page 6 to help you decide the dosage you need.

Ibuprofen (**Advil**, **Motrin** and others)
in tablet or liquid form for adult or child use

Dimetapp or other combination
decongestant and antihistamine preparation

Diphenhydramine (**Benadryl**)
or other oral antihistamine
for allergic reactions and itching rashes

Cough medication containing DM *(dextromethorphan)*

Dimenhydrinate (**Gravol**)
suppositories and tablets for nausea and vomiting

Anaesthetic mouth spray such as **Chloraseptic** and lozenges of any type to soothe a sore throat

Local anaesthetic spray and ointment
for cuts and scrapes such as **Bactine** or benzocaine (**Solarcaine**)

Antibiotic ointment such as **Polysporin**
for burns and scrapes

Antibiotic eye drops or ear drops such as **Polysporin**
for pink eye and ear infections

Antacid (**Maalox**, **Riopan**, **Tums**, **Rolaids**, etc.)
for heartburn or indigestion

Check with your pharmacist for advice about substitutions to this list.

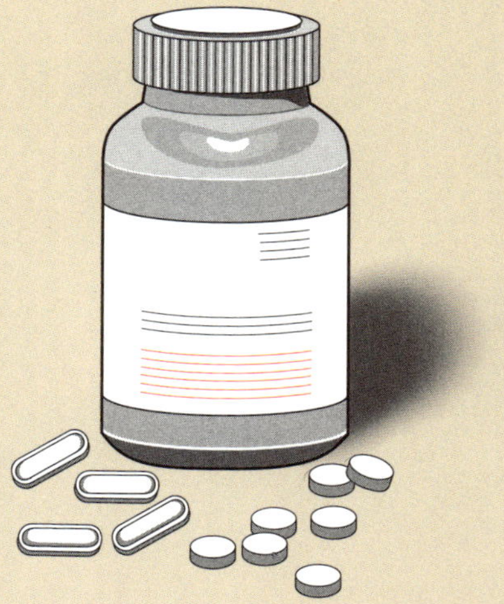

How to use this book

This self-help book has been designed to assist people, with otherwise good health, to deal with some of life's common health problems. It is not designed to replace your doctor. It was written to give people some of the knowledge needed to better treat these common problems. This book will give you advice that you may receive from a doctor without the inconvenience and expense of an office or emergency room visit.

People with serious medical problems such as severe lung disease, heart disease, kidney failure, diabetes, liver disease, cancer or AIDS will frequently need to seek medical assistance earlier to reduce the chance that the chronic or serious medical condition might get worse. If you are unwell and cannot cope, you must see your family doctor or go to the hospital.

When we refer to children in this book we mean anyone under 16 years of age.

To use this book properly:

1. Select your topic and read that section thoroughly, from start to finish, before using the advice given.
2. Re-evaluate how you or your child is doing regularly during the illness.
3. Consult your doctor or go to the hospital immediately should you or your child's condition be rapidly changing for the worse. Anyone who appears very ill should see a doctor promptly.
4. Read this book over BEFORE you need it in an urgent situation. **THE INFORMATION PAGES** will help you make decisions about products you may wish to buy from your local pharmacy.

Initially some charts in this book may look difficult. All questions are answered by a "YES" or "NO". Just follow the arrows and you will find it very user friendly.

What do you need?

You must be genuinely interested

Keep this book in a handy place where you can easily find it whenever you have a health problem. Use this book to improve your skills in caring for yourself and your family. It would also be a good idea to **TAKE THIS BOOK** with you when you are travelling or on vacation. Proper and timely use of this book may save you from making unnecessary hospital or doctor visits.

You will need some tools

Making wise decisions about health problems is easier when you have the right tools. **YOU NEED A GOOD THERMOMETER.** Your hand on someone's forehead can give false information: The best thermometer to buy is an electronic digital model. A glass thermometer is the second best option. If you are using glass thermometers you will need one for oral and one for rectal use. Washing a thermometer in hot water may cause it to break. Temperature strips are not accurate and should not be trusted. Tympanic or ear thermometers are more difficult to get accurate results from.
See page 3 for more information about taking a temperature.

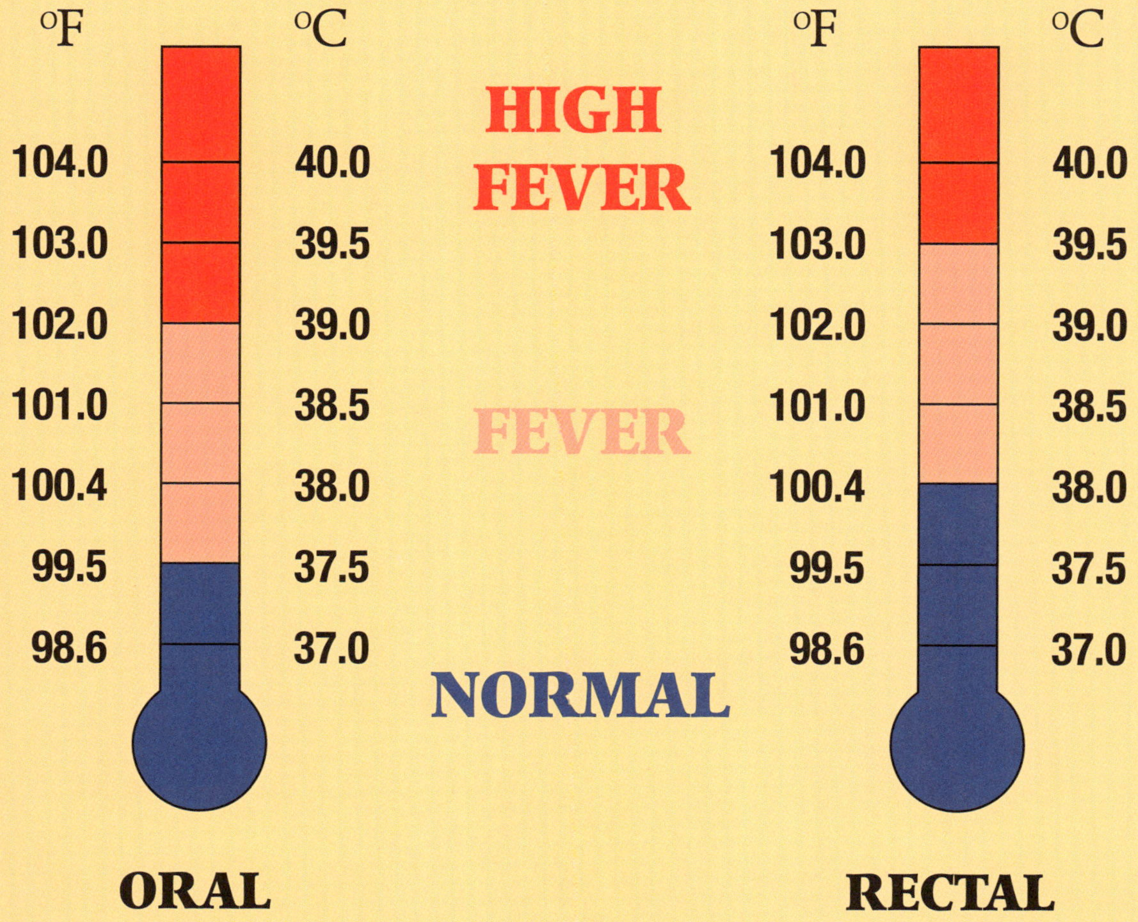

"Did you know that fever may help us fight infections? However, we often feel better if we treat the fever".

Fever What you should know about fever

A fever, or the elevation of the body's temperature, is usually a symptom of infection and it is not usually a problem in itself. If the fever is not causing a problem, you do not need to treat it. Fever is one of the ways we fight infection. However, we often feel a lot better when our fever is treated. A fever should prompt a parent to watch for a source of infection. Viral infections do not have specific treatments. If the fever is high or prolonged despite home therapy, then a visit to your family doctor is advised. Children under 3 months of age, anyone on chemotherapy, anyone with a serious ongoing disease, and those who have had recent surgery should seek medical advice about all fevers.

What is fever?

	Normal	Fever	High Fever
Temperature Orally (taken by mouth)	up to 37.5°C (99.5°F)	37.5 - 39.0°C 99.5 - 102°F	over 39.0°C over 102°F
Temperature Rectally (taken by rectum)	up to 38.0°C (100.4°F)	38.0 - 39.5°C 100.4 - 103°F	over 39.5°C over 103°F

Keep in mind that body temperature may elevate with exercise, with overdressing, after a hot bath, or as a result of very hot weather. Be sure to recheck a temperature you are unsure of in 30 to 60 minutes.

How to take a temperature

When taking a temperature you must have the right equipment. You cannot depend on the feel of a forehead with your hand to determine someone's temperature accurately. As discussed on page 1 we recommend you obtain either an electronic or glass thermometer. Temperatures are best taken rectally or orally. You should take a look at the thermometer before use and note how you have to rotate the glass to see the mercury or alcohol. As noted above, the oral temperature may be lower than the rectal temperature because the mouth is cooled by breathing. Be sure you shake the glass thermometer down below 37°C or 99°F before using it.

AN ORAL TEMPERATURE may be used in older children or adults. Oral temperatures may be falsely high or low depending on recent hot or cold drinks. Wait about 10 minutes after drinking to take an oral temperature.

A RECTAL TEMPERATURE is more accurate and should be performed if possible. This is important in young children who may not cooperate for an oral temperature or may bite a glass thermometer.
Taking a rectal temperature does not hurt the child.

How to take a RECTAL temperature

1. Lay the child over your lap.
2. Lubricate the thermometer with Vaseline or other lubricant.
3. Hold the thermometer about 1 inch from the end to prevent insertion more than 1 inch. Ease it into the rectum. Do not force it.
4. Read the temperature after 2 minutes with a glass thermometer, or when the electronic thermometer "beeps".

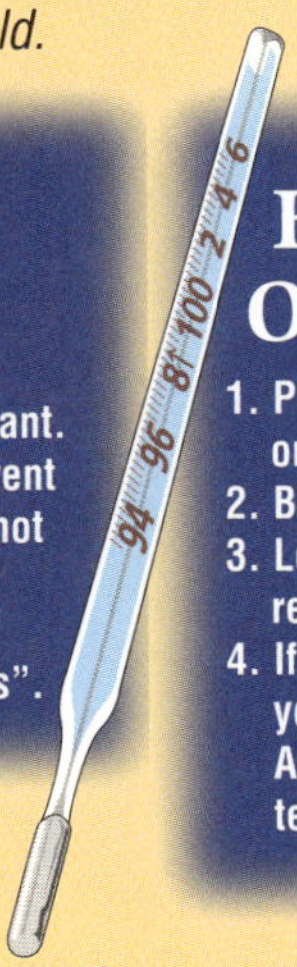

How to take an ORAL temperature

1. Place the oral thermometer under the tongue on one side or the other towards the back of the mouth.
2. Be certain that it is being held by the lips, not by the teeth.
3. Leave the thermometer in place for 3 minutes before reading the temperature.
4. If the child cannot nose breathe because of congestion, you can suction out the nose first with a small suction bulb. Ask your pharmacist. Mouth breathing while taking the temperature will falsely lower the temperature.

★ ***We feel that armpit temperatures and skin temperature strips are inaccurate and are not advised.***

Fever

See page 3 to learn how to measure a temperature.

START HERE

A FEVER IS SUSPECTED

Take the temperature now!

↓

Oral temperature less than 37.5˚C (99.5˚F) ?
Rectal temperature less than 38.0˚C (100.4˚F) ?

YES → **REPEAT TEMPERATURE IN 4 HOURS** and return to previous page

NO ↓

Is your child less than 3 months old?
Does the child or adult have a serious medical illness?

YES → Give medication for fever *(see page 6 and 78)* then **GO TO YOUR DOCTOR** *or* **GO TO THE HOSPITAL NOW**

NO ↓

Does your child look severely ill?
Do you or your child complain of severe headache?
Is your child hallucinating or acting confused?

YES → Give medication for fever *(see page 6 and 78)* then **GO TO YOUR DOCTOR** *or* **GO TO THE HOSPITAL NOW**

NO ↓

Is the child happy and acting well?

YES → Encourage drinking of water and juices then measure the temperature in 4 hours

NO ↓

Use HOME SUGGESTIONS

↓

2 HOURS AFTER TREATMENT:
Is the temperature greater than 39˚C (102˚F) Rectal or 38.5˚C (101˚F) Oral?
or **Does the child or adult look very ill?**

YES → **GO TO YOUR DOCTOR** *or* **GO TO THE HOSPITAL**

NO ↓

Has there been a fever for more than 3 days?

YES → **GO TO YOUR DOCTOR** *or* **GO TO THE HOSPITAL**

NO ↓

Continue HOME SUGGESTIONS and review in 4 hours

↓

Return to previous symptom page or refer to pages about other symptoms

Home Suggestions

1 When your child has a fever, dress the child lightly and don't cover with blankets.

2 If the child or adult starts to shiver, dress him/her warmly until it stops, then dress lightly again.

3 Give acetaminophen (**Tylenol** and others) every 4 hours if the child or adult is uncomfortable or if the child's temperature is high (see chart on page 6 for proper dose). Ibuprofen (**Advil**, **Motrin** and others) may be used instead of acetaminophen. Ibuprofen is taken every 6 to 8 hours. Do not use ASA (**Aspirin** and others) in anyone under 20 years of age (see page 78).

4 If the child or adult vomits the medication given for pain or fever, you can use acetaminophen suppositories (medication given rectally) instead. Ask your pharmacist for help.

5 We suggest that you do not sponge bath your feverish child. Sponge baths tend to reduce the temperature for only a short time and make many children unhappy and uncomfortable. Bathing may also cause shivering which will raise the temperature again.

6 Encourage the child or adult to drink plenty of liquids. Fluid losses are increased with fever.

7 Take the temperature every 4 hours and certainly if you feel the fever is worse.

8 If the child or adult complains of a sore throat, cough, earache or other problems, please review these topics as well.

Medication information

Acetaminophen dosing chart

Using an age chart to decide upon dosage will always underdose heavier children in the age group. If you are comfortable with doing some basic math, you can figure out a precise dose for your child if you know his/her weight. Physicians decide whether or not a proper dose has been given by multiplying the child's weight in kilograms by 15, or the weight in pounds by 6.5. This gives the total milligrams of acetaminophen that is needed per dose. You then can choose the dose of liquid or number of tablets needed from the chart below.

For example: A child weighs 20 lbs X 6.5 mg/lb = 130 mg.
This may be rounded down to 120 mg for a convenient dose.
You should check the dosage calculated before giving this to your child.

WEIGHT Pounds	Kilograms	DOSE every 4 hours	80 mg/1 ml 5 ml=1 tsp	160 mg/5 ml	80 mg tabs	160 mg tabs Junior	325 mg tabs Regular	500 mg tabs X-strength
7-10 lbs	<5 kg	40 mg	.5 ml	1.25 ml	1/2 tab			
10-18 lbs	5-8 kg	80 mg	1.0 ml	2.5 ml	1 tab	1/2 tab		
18-26 lbs	8-12 kg	120 mg	1.5 ml	4.0 ml	1 1/2 tabs			
26-35 lbs	12-16 kg	160 mg	2.0 ml	5.0 ml	2 tabs	1 tab	1/2 tab	
35-45 lbs	16-20 kg	240 mg	3.0 ml	7.5 ml	3 tabs	1 1/2 tabs		
45-55 lbs	20-25 kg	320 mg	4.0 ml	10.0 ml	4 tabs	2 tabs	1 tab	
55-65 lbs	25-30 kg	400 mg	5.0 ml	12.5 ml	5 tabs	2 1/2 tabs		
65-80 lbs	30-36 kg	480 mg		15.0 ml	6 tabs	3 tabs	1 1/2 tabs	1 tab
80-95 lbs	36-44 kg	560 mg		17.5 ml	7 tabs	3 1/2 tabs	1 3/4 tabs	1 tab
95-145 lbs	44-65 kg	650 mg				4 tabs	2 tabs	1 1/2 tabs
145 lbs +	65 kg +	650-1000 mg					2-3 tabs	2 tabs

Use the weight chart and go across to find the most convenient form of acetaminophen. This will help you choose which type to purchase.

Ibuprofen dosing chart

As outlined in the acetaminophen chart instructions the dose of ibuprofen should depend on the individuals weight. If you use age as the determinant of dose you will underdose all the larger children in that age group. The dose of ibuprofen is 10 mg per kilogram (2 lbs) of body weight and can be given every 6 to 8 hours.

WEIGHT Pounds	Kilograms	DOSE every 6 hours	100 mg/5 ml 1 tsp=5 ml	200 mg tabs
7-10 lbs	<5 kg	40 mg	2 ml or 1/2 tsp	
10-18 lbs	5-8 kg	60 mg	3 ml or 1/2 tsp	
18-25 lbs	8-12 kg	100 mg	5 ml or 1 tsp	1/2 tab
26-30 lbs	12-14 kg	140 mg	7 ml or 1 1/2 tsp	3/4 tab
30-35 lbs	14-16 kg	150 mg	8 ml or 1 1/2 tsp	3/4 tab
35-45 lbs	16-20 kg	170 mg	9 ml or 1 3/4 tsp	3/4 tab
45-55 lbs	20-25 kg	200 mg	10 ml or 2 tsp	1 tab
55-75 lbs	25-35 kg	300 mg	15 ml or 3 tsp	1 1/2 tabs
75-125 lbs	35-60 kg	400 mg	20 ml or 4 tsp	2 tabs
125-150 lbs	60-70 kg	up to 600 mg		up to 3 tabs
150-200 lbs	70-90 kg	up to 800 mg		up to 4 tabs
200 lbs+	90 kg +	800 mg		4 tabs

Cough & Cold and "the Flu"

CHILDREN Possible Symptoms:

- runny nose
- congested nose
- cough
- swollen glands
- sore throat
- sore ears
- watery eyes
- cough
- fever
- irritability
- reduced appetite
- interrupted sleep

Summary:

First of all, it is important to understand that the average child gets 6 to 10 colds per year. Many of these colds may be mild and go unnoticed by parents. Colds are caused by viruses. **Antibiotics will have no effect on the viruses that cause colds.** The symptoms of a cold can be treated very successfully at home. Having a sick child at home can be distressing; however, most children with colds do not need to see a physician. Occasional vomiting, or throwing up, after a coughing spell is common and is not a serious symptom. A cold may cause a dry cough which can last up to 2 or 3 weeks after other symptoms have passed. Sore throats and earaches are also commonly associated with colds. (see pages 11 and 14) .

Cough & Cold and "The Flu"
children

START HERE

COMMON COLD SYMPTOMS

↓

Is your child less than 3 months old?
or
Does your child have a fever above 39.5˚C (103˚F) Rectal or 39˚C (102˚F) Oral?
or
Does the child look severely ill?
or
Does your child have difficulty breathing?
or
Does your child have severe difficulty swallowing?

YES → Use fever medication if required (page 6 and 78) and **GO TO YOUR DOCTOR *or* GO TO THE HOSPITAL NOW**

H

NO ↓

Use HOME SUGGESTIONS

↓

Has there been a fever (greater than 37.5˚C or 99.5˚F) for more than 3 days?
or
Is there poor intake of fluids?
or
Is the child coughing up green coloured sputum?

YES → **GO TO YOUR DOCTOR *or* GO TO THE HOSPITAL**

NO ↓

Continue HOME SUGGESTIONS Reassess your child from the top of this chart every 4 hours.

Home Suggestions

Remember, there is no cure for the common cold.
Antibiotics will not shorten the cold or cure it.
You can, however, help your child to feel better by following these suggestions:

1. If your child has a fever see the "**FEVER**" section on pages 3-6.

2. Use acetaminophen (**Tylenol** and others) or ibuprofen (**Advil**, **Motrin** and others) to control fever and relieve discomfort. See page 6 for acetaminophen and ibuprofen dosage. ASA (**Aspirin** and others) should not be given to anyone under 20 years of age with a viral illness. See page 78 for an explanation.

3. For a runny nose: If your child is able, encourage him/her to blow his nose. Don't discourage sniffling. It's actually a good way to clear the nose. It does not push infection into the ears or sinuses.
   For very young children who cannot blow and clear their nose themselves, use a rubber bulb to gently suction out mucus.
   Using a saline nasal spray, purchased from your pharmacy, can help dry the nose. Do not use decongestant nasal sprays for children. They may cause problems.

4. For a plugged nose: While your child is lying on his/her back, drip 3 drops of warm tap water in each nostril. After 1 minute, have the child blow his/her nose or use the bulb suction as described above. Repeat as often as necessary.

5. Oral decongestant medication or combination medications, like **Dimetapp**, can help dry up a runny nose and improve sleep. see page 74. However, do not use decongestant medications where there is severe heart disease, poorly controlled high blood pressure, or severe asthma. Antihistamines are not recommended for children under 2 years.

6. Cough syrups with "DM" (dextromethorphan) may be helpful for a dry cough if getting to sleep or concentrating at school is a problem. You don't want to suppress a wet or loose cough because this type of cough is clearing the mucus from the chest. "DM" should not be given to a child if he/she is having breathing problems (e.g. asthma or croup).
   Do not give "DM" to children under 1 year.

7. Sipping warm drinks can help loosen a cough. Warm water with sugar or warm juice such as lemonade or even chicken soup are good examples.

Home Suggestions

8 A lozenge may help a sore and dry throat if the child is old enough to have a hard candy. These come in many flavours and varieties. Use one that your child likes. Expensive lozenges are not necessary. Hard candies of any kind work well.

9 Do not expose your child to cigarette smoke.

10 Your child should not exercise or play hard, but should get plenty of rest. Make sure she/he drinks extra fluids. Use a cool mist humidifier in your home if you have one.

11 **Do not stop breast feeding**. Feed your child smaller portions more often if necessary.

12 Frequent hand washing can decrease the spread of infection.

Sore Throat

CHILDREN Possible Symptoms:

- pain in the throat
- difficulty swallowing
- refusal to eat and drink
- fever
- red throat or pus on the tonsils
- swollen glands in the neck
- other cold symptoms

Summary:

Keep in mind that sore throats are a common childhood problem. Viral infections (the common cold) is often the cause of the sore throat. Most sore throats **DO NOT RESPOND TO ANTIBIOTICS**. The pain and discomfort will usually ease within 48 hours. Indeed, many sore throats will feel better after some simple therapy at home. Follow the flow chart to help you decide if you should take your child to the doctor.

Sore Throat
children

START HERE

SORE THROAT

↓

Is your child less than 3 months old?
or
Is there a fever greater than 39.5°C (103°F) Rectal or 39°C (102°F) Oral?

YES → Use fever medication if required (page 6 and 78) and **GO TO YOUR DOCTOR *or* GO TO THE HOSPITAL NOW** (H)

NO ↓

Is the child drooling more than usual? *or*
Is the child's chin pushed forward? *or*
Is the child having extreme difficulty swallowing? *or*
Is the child having difficulty breathing? *or*
Does the child look severely ill?

YES → **GO TO THE HOSPITAL NOW** (H)

NO ↓

Does your child have a severe sore throat and enlarged glands without other cough or cold symptoms?

YES → **GO TO YOUR DOCTOR *or* GO TO THE HOSPITAL**

NO ↓

Use HOME SUGGESTIONS

and review this chart from the top every 4 hours

↓

AFTER THE FIRST 48 HOURS:
Check this chart from the top and decide if:

↓

The symptoms are getting worse? *or*
Is a rash developing?

YES → **GO TO YOUR DOCTOR *or* GO TO THE HOSPITAL**

NO ↓

Continue HOME SUGGESTIONS

Home Suggestions

1. If your child has a fever with a sore throat, please see the "**FEVER**" section on pages 3-6.
2. You may give your child acetaminophen (**Tylenol** and others) for pain. Ibuprofen (**Advil**, **Motrin** and others) may be used instead. See page 6 for acetaminophen and ibuprofen dosage. See page 78 for further information and advice about pain medication. ASA (**Aspirin** and others) is not to be given to anyone 20 years and younger.
3. Make sure your child has plenty of cool drinks which will help soothe the throat.
4. Gargles or anesthetic preparations can help reduce the pain of a sore throat and make eating less troublesome. A salt-water gargle (1/2 to 1 teaspoon of salt in 8 oz of warm water) may give some relief and can be used several times daily. Younger children may have trouble gargling and if they tend to swallow the mixture, reduce the salt content to 1/4 to 1/2 teaspoon. Avoid gargling at all if it is too painful, or if the child cannot gargle without choking.
   You can buy local anesthetic ("freezing" or "numbing") sprays (**Chloraseptic**) and gargles at your pharmacy. These medicines usually contain 0.5% phenol and a flavouring. We have found that children may eat more comfortably if these sprays are used before meals.
   Swallowing one or two tablespoons of corn syrup may also soothe a sore throat.
5. For children over age 1 year, give a teaspoon of honey 3 times daily.
   DO NOT GIVE HONEY TO CHILDREN UNDER 1 YEAR OF AGE.
6. If your child is old enough to have a hard candy, allow him/her to suck on a lozenge. One does not have to buy expensive lozenges. Hard candies of almost any kind will work well.
7. Give your child plenty to drink. Children may find it more comfortable to swallow soft foods and soups for the first few days.
8. Frequent hand washing can decrease the spread of infection.

Earache

CHILDREN
Possible Symptoms:

- earache
- poor hearing
- drainage from the ear
- fever
- sore glands around the ear or in the neck
- pain when the ear is tugged.
- itchy ears
- infants may pull on the ear

Summary:

You can have an ear infection which occurs outside the ear drum in the ear canal or behind the ear drum. Ear canal infections may develop after a day of swimming or water play ("swimmer's ear"). Similarly, the ear canal is more likely to become infected if it has been irritated by using cotton-swabs.

Infections behind the ear drum, called middle ear infections, can result from congestion during a cold or flu when the Eustachian tube plugs and the normal drainage to the throat is blocked. Middle ear infections are uncommon in children under 6 months of age. Breast-fed babies seem to have fewer ear infections.

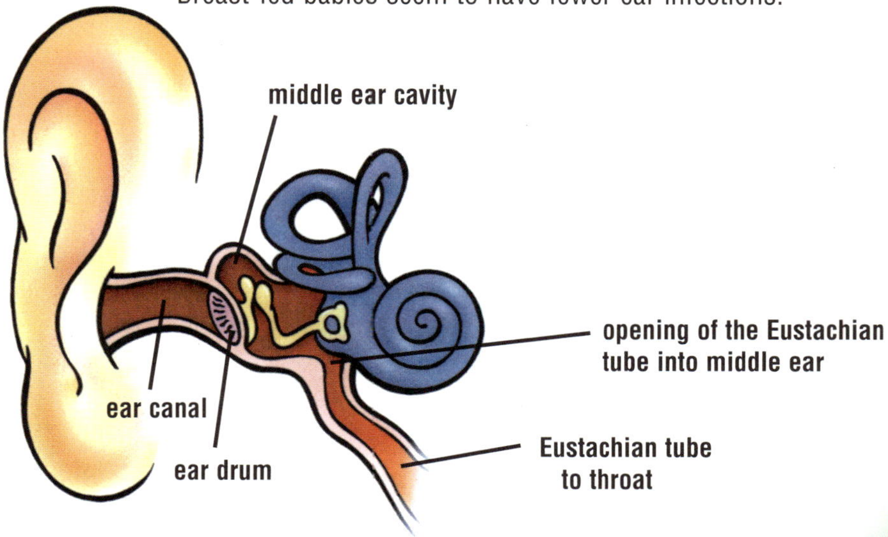

Earache
children

START HERE

PAIN IN OR AROUND THE EAR

↓

Is your child less than 3 months old?
or
Does the child have a fever above 39.5˚C (103˚F) Rectal or 39˚C (102˚F) Oral?
or
Is there a discharge or drainage from the ear?
or
Is your child very sleepy and weak?
or
Does your child have a severe headache, or complain of severe pain on moving his/her neck?

YES → Use fever medication if required (page 6 and 78) and **GO TO YOUR DOCTOR *or* GO TO THE HOSPITAL NOW**

NO ↓

Is the pain made worse by quick tugs or by pulling lightly on the ear lobe?

YES → **Possible ear canal infection "Swimmer's Ear"** → Use HOME SUGGESTIONS and special SUGGESTIONS "B" (see page 17)

NO ↓

Possible middle ear infection

↓

Use HOME SUGGESTIONS and special SUGGESTIONS "A" (see page 16)

↓

Is there still pain or fever after 12 to 24 hours therapy?

YES → **GO TO YOUR DOCTOR *or* GO TO THE HOSPITAL**

NO ↓

Continue HOME SUGGESTIONS for one week

Home Suggestions

*If your child has a fever, please see the "**FEVER**" section on pages 3-6.*

1 Give your child acetaminophen (**Tylenol** and others) or Ibuprofen (**Advil**, **Motrin** and others) for pain. See page 78 for more details about pain medication. See page 6 for acetaminophen and ibuprofen dosage. Do not use ASA (**Aspirin** and others) in anyone under 20 years of age (see page 78 for an explanation).

2 Your child can be made more comfortable by putting a warm cloth on the ear for 20 minutes several times daily.

3 Sometimes putting warm oil drops in the ear canal may give some relief. You can buy **Auralgan** drops or simply use mineral oil, cooking oil or olive oil. Heat the oil in warm water. Do not boil the water. Make sure you test the temperature of the oil drops on your skin before placing it in your child's ear.

4 If you are breast feeding, do not stop, but try to nurse so the child is in an upright position. If necessary, feed smaller amounts more often.

5 Do not expose your child to cigarette smoke.

6 Read about Fever, Cough and Colds, and Sore Throat if necessary.

Special suggestions "A"

When your child has middle ear pain:

1 Encourage your child to "pop" his/her ears by blowing against a pinched nose. Get him/her to do this several times daily.

2 Doctors now know that most middle ear infections do not need to be treated with antibiotics. Use pain medication early. Night time visits to the emergency department are usually unnecessary.

3 Repeated ear infections may be prevented. Ask your Family Doctor.

Home Suggestions

Special suggestions "B"

When your child has an ear canal infection or "Swimmer's Ear":

1 Keep the child's ear dry for at least 7 days. Avoid swimming or water play that involves getting water in the ears. A few drops of a drying agent will help the ear dry faster. Burosol or a mixture of 1 tablespoon of vinegar in 1 tablespoon of warm water makes a good drying agent.

2 This is an infection which may improve with the non-prescription antibiotic drop (**Polysporin**). Use 2 drops 4 times daily.

3 **DO NOT TRY TO CLEAN THE EAR OUT OR PUT OBJECTS, SUCH AS COTTON SWABS, INTO THE EAR.**

4 If your child gets infections of the ear canal over and over again you may want to try and prevent these before symptoms appear. Placing a couple of drops of cooking, olive or mineral oil in the canal before swimming or placing a couple of drops of antibiotic solution (**Polysporin**) in the canal after a day of swimming may help to prevent repeat infections.

Vomiting or "Stomach Flu"

CHILDREN
Possible Symptoms:

- vomiting ("throwing up")

And some or all of the following:

- abdominal pain
- cramps
- fever
- diarrhea

Summary:

Vomiting, or "throwing up", is the forceful exit of what is in the stomach by way of the mouth. Infants often spit up, but in a gentle way; this is different from vomiting. The most common cause of vomiting is the "stomach flu", a viral illness. You can usually care for your child by changing his/her diet and letting the symptoms run their course. Your child does not usually require medication to treat the "stomach flu". If you can keep your child drinking small amounts frequently, you should not need to see your doctor. This is especially true if the child looks well between episodes of vomiting.

Vomiting or "Stomach Flu"

children

START HERE

VOMITING OR "THROWING UP"

↓

Is your child less than 6 months old?

or

Does your child have a fever above 39.5˚C (103˚F) Rectal or 39˚C (102˚F) Oral?

or

Do you suspect poisoning?

or

Does your child have severe stomach pain?

or

Is your child severely ill between vomiting episodes?

or

Do you suspect a head injury?

or

Is the child diabetic?

or

Could the child be pregnant?

or

Is there evidence of dehydration?
See "A", page 20, for details.

YES → **GO TO YOUR DOCTOR *or* GO TO THE HOSPITAL NOW**

NO ↓

Use HOME SUGGESTIONS

↓

Is your child unable to drink fluids and has there been regular hourly vomiting for more than 4 hours?

YES → **GO TO YOUR DOCTOR *or* GO TO THE HOSPITAL NOW**

NO ↓

Continue HOME SUGGESTIONS

Review this chart from the top every 2 hours.

Home Suggestions

Ⓐ Your child may be dehydrated if:

1 There are fewer than 4 wet diapers per day or the child has not urinated during the last 8 hours.
2 There are no tears when your child cries.
3 Your child's mouth is dry or the eyes are sunken.
4 Your child is dizzy when he/she stands.
5 Your child is very sleepy and weak.

Important feeding advice for children of all ages

If your child vomits once, give him/her a 2 hour break from food and fluids to allow the stomach to settle. If he/she vomits again, you must take action to avoid dehydration. Remember the key to caring for a vomiting child is to give small amounts of liquid often. This will usually control the vomiting. Use a medicine dropper, spoon or cup if it helps your child take the fluids. ***Give 1oz. every 20 to 30 minutes.***

Many experts would advise that you immediately stop all food and fluids and give oral "rehydration" drinks such as **Gastrolyte** or **Pedialyte** until vomiting stops. We agree that this is ideal to prevent dehydration, but many parents have found that the unpleasant taste of these liquids can make this difficult. You can add unsweetened drink crystals to help improve the taste. Some people make freeze-pops from this mixture for their kids to suck on when ill.

If the vomiting and/or diarrhea is mild, we feel it is reasonable to start with clear fluids. This includes water, apple juice, pear juice, flattened ginger ale and popsicles. If there is diarrhea, make sure that you dilute the juices with an equal amount of water. If the vomiting continues, then we suggest that you switch to the "rehydration" drinks. **A clear fluid diet is only acceptable for 24 hours. After that period you should start using rehydration drinks**.

If you are unable to get these fluids into your child and regular vomiting and/or diarrhea continues for more than 4 hours, you should see a doctor. Children with both vomiting and diarrhea must be watched closely for signs of dehydration (see above).

How much fluid should you give your child?

Age	1 year and under	1 - 2 years	over 2 years
Amount	15 ml *or* 1 tbsp *or* 1/2 oz → every 15 minutes	30 ml *or* 2 tbsp *or* 1 oz → every 15-20 minutes	30-60 ml *or* 2-4 tbsp *or* 1-2 oz → every 15-20 minutes

This is a guide and must be adjusted according to whether fluid losses have been mild or severe.
Even if the child is vomiting, continue to give the fluids.
The child is always keeping some of the swallowed fluids.

Home Suggestions

How to care for breast-fed babies

1 **Do not stop breast feeding!** Breast milk is a natural fluid that is easily and rapidly digested. Even if your baby is vomiting, he/she will absorb some nutrients and fluid before it comes back up.

Nurse for half the length of the time but twice as often as usual. If vomiting continues, reduce the nursing time and feed your child more often. Remember that a sick child becomes tired quickly. For comfort you may have to express some milk and offer a less full breast for feeding. Make sure you read "**Important feeding advice for children of all ages**" on page 20.

2 If your child has a fever, please see the "**FEVER**" section on pages 3-6. If your child has vomited up the medication, you can use suppositories (medication taken rectally) which contains acetaminophen. Ask your pharmacist to help you purchase the right product.

3 Do not give any medication for vomiting to children under 3 years of age. We find that dimenhydrinate (**Gravol**), which is frequently used in older children and adults, is usually unnecessary and we have found it to be unhelpful in younger children.

4 Vomiting which is irregular or infrequent and allows your child to drink some fluids between episodes is not as serious as hourly vomiting. Nevertheless, if irregular or infrequent vomiting should continue for more than 24 hours, you should visit your doctor.

5 If your child is normally eating solid food and has not vomited for at least 4 to 6 hours, you are quite safe and wise to reintroduce food. Some experts suggest that you start with bland foods such as rice, cereal, strained bananas, applesauce, bread, crackers, etc. Our advice is to give the child healthy food that he/she likes to eat as long as it does not make them sick again. Gradually return to a normal diet within 1 or 2 days.

6 Frequent hand washing can decrease the spread of infection.

THE NEXT PAGE HAS ADVICE FOR FORMULA-FED AND OLDER CHILDREN. FOR A HOMEMADE REHYDRATION DRINK SEE PAGE 48.

Home Suggestions

How to care for formula-fed babies and older children

1 Make sure you read "**Important feeding advice for children of all ages**" (page 20).

2 If your child has a fever, please see the "**FEVER**" section on pages 3-6. Suppositories (medication given rectally) containing acetaminophen can be used when medication taken by mouth won't stay down. Ask your pharmacist to help you purchase the right product.

3 Do not give any medication for vomiting to children under 3 years of age. **Gravol** which is frequently used in older children and adults is usually unnecessary and we have found it to be unhelpful in younger children. A 25 mg dose by mouth or as a rectal suppository can be used in children over age 3.

4 Vomiting which is irregular or infrequent and allows your child to drink some fluids between episodes is not as serious as hourly vomiting. Nevertheless, if irregular or infrequent vomiting should continue for more than 24 hours, you should visit your doctor.

5 If your child has not vomited in the last 6 hours, you can restart milk and foods. Many experts suggest that you start with bland foods such as rice, cereal, bread, crackers, potatoes, etc. Our advice is to give the child healthy food that he/she like as long as it does not make him/her sick again. Gradually return to a normal diet in 1 to 2 days.

6 Frequent hand washing can decrease the spread of infection.

FOR A HOMEMADE REHYDRATION DRINK SEE PAGE 48.
HOW MUCH FLUID SHOULD YOU GIVE YOUR CHILD? SEE PAGE 20.

Diarrhea

CHILDREN
Possible Symptoms:

- loose, frequent, watery bowel movements
- cramps
- reduced appetite
- nausea
- vomiting
- fever
- body aches

Summary:

Diarrhea is a common problem at any age. A sudden change in diet is a common cause of some short-lived loosening of bowel movements. The rapid onset of frequent, loose bowel movements without bleeding, however, is usually the result of a viral illness or "stomach flu". Mild diarrhea in a child whose intake of fluids and food remains normal is not usually serious and does not require a visit to the doctor. More serious diarrhea requires specific diet planning and close monitoring to make sure that dehydration does not develop. It may take from 7 to 10 days for bowel movements to return to normal. If the diarrhea contains blood, you should see a doctor.

Diarrhea
children

START HERE

DIARRHEA

↓

Is your child less than 6 months old? — YES → **GO TO YOUR DOCTOR *or* GO TO THE HOSPITAL NOW** (H)

NO ↓

Is your child vomiting? — YES → **SEE "VOMITING" page 18 then return to this page**

NO ↓

Has the child had fewer than 2 or 3 small, loose stools? — YES → **CONTINUE THE NORMAL DIET**

NO ↓

Use HOME SUGGESTIONS

↓

Check symptoms of dehydration; see "A" page 25 for details.
or
Are the bowel movements black or bloody?
or
Has there been a fever greater than 39.5˚C (103˚F) Rectal or 39˚C (102˚F) Oral?
or
Is there severe stomach pain?
or
Is your child severely ill, highly irritable very sleepy or very weak?
or
Is there severe diarrhea with bowel movements hourly for 4 hours?

— YES → **Use fever medication if required (page 6 and 78) and GO TO YOUR DOCTOR *or* GO TO THE HOSPITAL NOW** (H)

NO ↓

Continue HOME SUGGESTIONS

If diarrhea does not improve after two days see your doctor.

Home Suggestions

Ⓐ Your child may be dehydrated if:

1. Your child has not urinated for 8 hours.
2. There are no tears when your child cries.
3. Your child's mouth is dry or eyes are sunken.
4. Your child is dizzy when he/she stands.
5. Your child is very sleepy and weak.

General treatment suggestions for children with diarrhea

If your child has a fever, please see the "**FEVER**" section on pages 3-6.

Your goal in taking care of a child with diarrhea is to make sure he/she is getting enough to eat and drink so he/she do not develop dehydration. Otherwise, there is no specific treatment for a viral diarrhea.

Breast or formula fed children

Don't stop breast feeding. Whenever possible, maintain the child's intake of solid and liquid food. If the child's stools are very watery or frequent, you should give extra fluids between feedings. Sometimes using a spoon or a medicine dropper can help get the child to take the fluid. Many experts would recommend using oral rehydration drinks such as **Gastrolyte** or **Pedialyte** immediately to prevent dehydration. We agree that this is ideal; however, the taste of these products may make it difficult to give these fluids in adequate amounts if the child is not that thirsty. We suggest that water or dilute juice (add equal parts of water and juice) be used for a short period of time for mild and infrequent diarrhea. If vomiting is present or the diarrhea is persistent or severe, we suggest you use the rehydration drinks immediately. If the diarrhea has been present for 5 to 7 days, you may want to try and see if a lactose-free or soya-based formula helps to settle the problem. (Pump your breast-milk in the meantime so as to preserve the supply.) If you feel that your child is not keeping up with the fluid he/she is losing you should see a doctor.

The most important thing is to watch for signs of dehydration (see top of the page).

Older children

If milk and a normal solid food diet are tolerated, continue to feed normally. You should add additional fluids. Many experts advise the immediate use of oral rehydration drinks such as **Gastrolyte** or **Pedialyte** at this time. We agree that this is ideal and the best way to prevent dehydration. However, some children do not take these drinks well due to an unpleasant taste. You can improve them by adding unsweetened drink crystals.

Home Suggestions

We feel for mild and infrequent diarrhea it is safe to use clear liquids that the child enjoys and will take more easily. Juices should be diluted with an equal amount of water.

Soups (chicken soup or consomme), or flattened ginger-ale can be used for a short period of time. **Remember that any clear liquid diet is only acceptable for 24 hours**.

After that period, one should be using rehydration drinks and restarting solids.

We recommend your child be given a **minimum of 3 to 6 oz (90 to 180 mls) per hour**.

Sometimes using a spoon or a medicine dropper can help get the child to take the fluids.

When you are reintroducing food, some experts recommend that you start with bland foods such a rice, cereal, strained bananas, mashed potatoes, bread, etc. Our advice is to give the child healthy food that he/she likes as long as it does not make him/her sick again.

Gradually return to a normal diet in 1 to 2 days.

If the diarrhea is prolonged for 5 to 7 days, a lactose-free milk or soya-based formula may be tried for several days to see if the diarrhea slows.

If you are unable to get your child to drink well or you feel you are not keeping up with the fluid losses, you should see a doctor.

FOR A HOMEMADE REHYDRATION DRINK SEE PAGE 48.

Constipation

CHILDREN
Possible Symptoms:

- infrequent bowel movements
- pain with bowel movements
- hard and pebble like stools
- unable to move bowels
- small tears in the anal canal (fissures)
- cramps

Summary:

Constipation has various definitions but if a child cannot pass his/her stool or if there is obvious pain on passing stool, then he/she needs some treatment. Children often need to strain to have a bowel movement. If it is not painful, this is not a concern. Like adults, children may have different bowel habits. A daily bowel movement is not necessary.

The hardness of the stool depends on the fibre and water intake as well as the general health of the child. Breast-fed children may not move their bowels more often than once every 7 days. During the first week of life however, one should expect a daily bowel movement. Any change in diet, especially a change from breast milk to formula or the introduction of cow's milk and solid food, may result in a temporary firming up of bowel movements. This change is usually self-correcting. Constipation does not cause fever.

Constipation
children

START HERE

POSSIBLE CONSTIPATION

↓

Are bowel movements soft? — **YES** → **NO TREATMENT REQUIRED**

NO ↓

Is there severe pain or fever?
or
Does the child look ill? — **YES** → **GO TO YOUR DOCTOR** *or* **GO TO THE HOSPITAL NOW**

NO ↓

Use HOME SUGGESTIONS

↓

Is the child still constipated? — **YES** → **GO TO YOUR DOCTOR**

NO ↓

Continue HOME SUGGESTIONS

Home Suggestions

Children under 6 months of age

Constipation is very rare in this age group and should your child seem constipated, you should visit your doctor.

Children 6 to 12 months of age

1 Encourage your baby to drink more water and fruit juices such as prune, pear, or apple. Give juices at full strength. Do not dilute the juice with water.

2 If your baby is eating solids, increase high fibre foods such as cereals (wheat bran), prunes, beans, and pears.

3 Encourage your child to be as active as possible. Exercise can really help this problem and improve your child's overall health.

4 Although mineral oil is sometimes recommended for this age group, we suggest that any **regular** use of laxatives should be given under the supervision of your doctor. Frequently children need some help to empty the rectum. Using a glycerin suppository or children's enema is a simple and effective treatment. If mineral oil is used, give 1-2 tablespoons (15-30 mls) at bedtime. Mineral oil is also available in a mixture of raspberry jelly called **Lansoyl**. An alternative to mineral oil is lactulose. Ask your pharmacist to help purchase any of these treatments for occasional constipation.

Children over 1 year of age

1 Encourage your child to drink more water and fruit juices like prune, pear and apple. Do not dilute juice with water.

2 Increase the fibre in your child's diet with bran, beans, peanut butter, etc. Increasing the quantity of fruits and vegetables your child eats may also help. See "**CONSTIPATION: ADULT**", page 41-44, for more detail.

3 If getting your child to eat foods rich in fibre is difficult, a psyllium fibre substitute may be tried. Try mixing one of these products, such as **Metamucil**, with orange juice or other foods to hide the taste. The smooth variety of **Metamucil** may be easier for a child to take.

4 Don't resort to laxatives, suppositories, or enemas too easily. These products are only useful for short-term relief. Constipation requires a long-term solution.

Home Suggestions

5 Laxatives should be used for short-term relief only. See your doctor if laxatives are needed on a regular basis. If your child is having trouble getting the bowel movement started, you can use a glycerin suppository or children's enema. If you are going to use a laxative by mouth, we suggest Milk of Magnesia. It is given in a 1 to 2 tablespoon (15-30 mls) dose once or twice daily. Mineral oil may also be used in a 1 to 2 tablespoon dose at bedtime. An alternative to mineral oil is lactulose. Please ask your pharmacist to help purchase the right product for your child.

6 If your child is toilet trained, try to establish a routine. This means putting the child on the toilet for 5 to 15 minutes at a regular time. Choosing a time which coincides with previous common times for bowel movements or planning these times after meals is a good idea. You will be most successful if you stay away from trying to get your child to use the toilet at stressful times of the day. These would include getting ready for school, just before going out of the house or just prior to bed.

Cough & Cold and "the Flu"

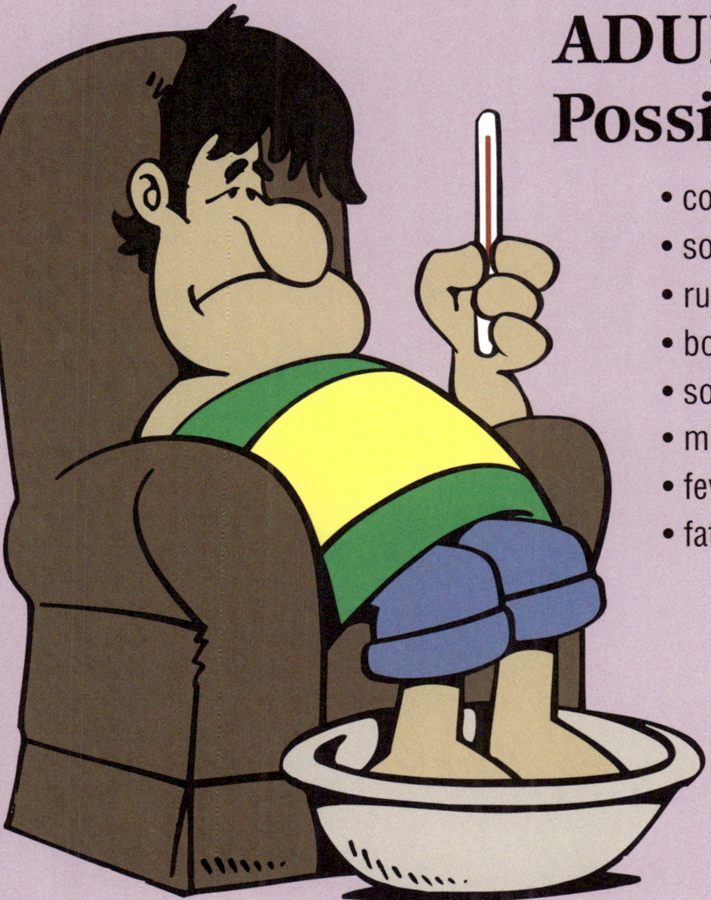

ADULT Possible Symptoms:

- cough
- sore throat
- runny nose
- body and joint aches
- sore swollen glands in the neck
- mild headache
- fever
- fatigue

"If you treat a cold it will last seven days; if you don't it will last about 1 week"
Somebody's Grandmother

Summary:

Colds are caused by viruses and do not have a specific treatment at this time. **Taking an antibiotic will not cure your cold.** The flow chart will help you decide if you need to see a doctor. During the course of a year, adults may get several colds which may vary in the amount of discomfort they cause. Some may go almost unnoticed, while others cause severe symptoms. **The very old, and those with lung disease, diabetes, heart disease, or other chronic illnesses may require a visit to the doctor sooner**. Normally, a cold will get better in 7 to 14 days whether you see a doctor or not. Some symptoms may last longer. A dry cough which may develop during a cold may last 2 to 3 weeks.

Cough & Cold and "the Flu"

adult

START HERE

COMMON COLD SYMPTOMS

Do you have a fever above 39.5°C (103°F) Rectal or 39°C (102°F) Oral?
or
Are you experiencing new shortness of breath?
or
Are you coughing up brown or bloody sputum?

YES → Use fever medication if required (page 6 and 78) and **GO TO THE HOSPITAL NOW**

NO ↓

Use HOME SUGGESTIONS

AFTER 3 DAYS:
Do you continue to cough up green mucus?
or
Is the cough getting worse?
or
Are you generally feeling worse?
or
Do you still have a fever?

YES → **GO TO YOUR DOCTOR**

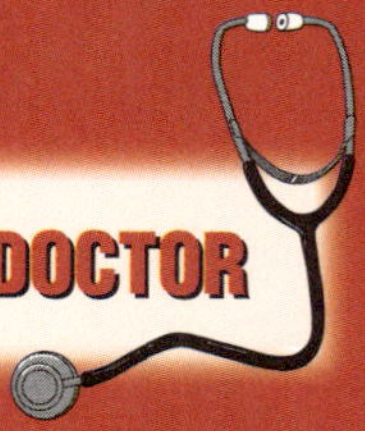

NO ↓

Continue HOME SUGGESTIONS

Home Suggestions

Remember, there is no cure for the common cold.
Antibiotics will not shorten the cold or cure it.
A cold will resolve within 7 to 10 days.
You can, however, do some things to help yourself or others feel better.

1 Rest and drink plenty of fluids to replace what you lose from a runny nose, cough and fever.

2 Use acetaminophen (**Tylenol** and others), ASA (**Aspirin** and others) or Ibuprofen (**Advil**, **Motrin** or others) for the fever, aches and pains. We do not recommend ASA for those under 20 years of age (see page 78 for further advice). See page 6 for acetaminophen and ibuprofen dosage.

3 Humidified air may help the cold symptoms. Use a cool mist humidifier. We suggest you avoid ultrasonic humidifiers and hot mist humidifiers.

4 Standing in a hot shower may help a congested head. Do this as often as you find helpful.

5 Drink hot liquids. These can help a congested nose, and loosen a cough. Chicken soup and hot lemon drinks are good suggestions.

6 You can try a decongestant for the head congestion and runny nose. Combination medications containing a decongestant and an antihistamine, such as **Dimetapp**, may improve sleep. Ask your pharmacist for assistance. See page 74.
Those with severe heart disease, poorly controlled blood pressure, angina, or asthma should not take decongestant medications.

7 Cough syrups with "DM" (dextromethorphan) may be used to ease a dry cough. You should not suppress all coughing. A loose or congested cough is helping you clear mucus from the air passages. A cough medicine may be used if you are not sleeping well or if you are finding it difficult to work because of the cough. "DM" containing products may make asthma worse. Use them with caution.

8 Coughs and sneezes spread infection. We recommend covering your mouth and nose, but most importantly, remember to wash your hands after you cough or you can spread the infection by touching people. Hand washing is very important in preventing the spread of your cold to other family members and co-workers.

9 Do not smoke or expose yourself to second hand smoke.

10 See "**SORE THROAT**" page 34 and "**FEVER**" page 3 if necessary.

Sore Throat

ADULT Possible Symptoms:

- sore throat
- pain on swallowing
- fever
- swollen neck glands
- hoarse voice or laryngitis
- red throat or pus on tonsils

Summary:

Most sore throats are part of a viral infection also causing a cough or cold. These viral infections cannot be cured with antibiotics. If you develop severe pain, high fever, a rash, or have a lot of difficulty swallowing, you should see a doctor. In most cases your sore throat will get better in 1 week or less. This flowchart will help you decide if you should see your doctor about your sore throat. The antibiotics do not help the pain immediately. Nighttime visits to the emergency department for antibiotics are usually unnecessary. Use the home suggestions for some early relief of the pain.

Sore Throat

adult

START HERE

SORE THROAT

(If accompanied by other cold symptoms see also "Cough & Cold")

Do you have a temperature greater than 39.5˚C (103˚F) Rectal or 39˚C (102˚F) Oral?

or

Are you having a lot of difficulty with swallowing or breathing?

or

Do you have a new skin rash?

or

Do you have a severe sore throat alone without the symptoms of a runny nose, cough or cold?

YES → **Use fever medication if required (page 6 and 78) and GO TO YOUR DOCTOR *or* GO TO THE HOSPITAL NOW**

NO ↓

Use HOME SUGGESTIONS

Are you swallowing more easily with home therapy?

NO → **GO TO YOUR DOCTOR**

YES ↓

Continue HOME SUGGESTIONS

Is the sore throat still severe or getting worse after 2 or 3 days?

YES → **GO TO YOUR DOCTOR**

NO ↓

Review this chart from the top in 24 hours.

Home Suggestions

1 Get plenty of rest and drink extra fluids.

2 Use acetaminophen (**Tylenol** and others), ASA (**Aspirin** and others) or Ibuprofen (**Advil**, **Motrin** and others) for pain and fever. We do not recommend ASA for those under 20 years of age. (see page 78 for further advice).
See page 6 for acetaminophen and ibuprofen dosage.

3 You may find that gargles or anesthetic ("numbing or freezing") medications may reduce the pain and help you to eat. Using a warm salt water gargle or double strength tea may also help give some relief. Combining 8 oz of warm water with 1 teaspoon of salt and 1 or 2 tablespoons of corn syrup or honey makes a soothing gargle. Products such as **Chloraseptic** which contain 0.5% phenol and flavouring may also be used with good results.

4 Suck on a lozenge or hard candy to help soothe your throat.

5 A cool-mist humidifier is helpful. We suggest that you avoid ultrasonic and hot-mist humidifiers.

6 Apply warm compresses to the sore neck glands for 30 minutes 4-6 times daily.

7 You may find that soft foods, soups and liquids are easier to swallow for the first 2-3 days.

8 If you have a hoarse voice (laryngitis), try to rest your voice. If your hoarse voice does not improve within 2 to 3 weeks you should see your doctor.

"Beware of the lone sore throat. A severe sore throat without cough, runny nose or chest congestion should be seen by a doctor."

Nausea, Vomiting or "Stomach Flu"

ADULT
Possible Symptoms:

- nausea (upset stomach)
- vomiting ("throwing up")

And some or all of the following:

- diarrhea
- fever
- headache
- dehydration

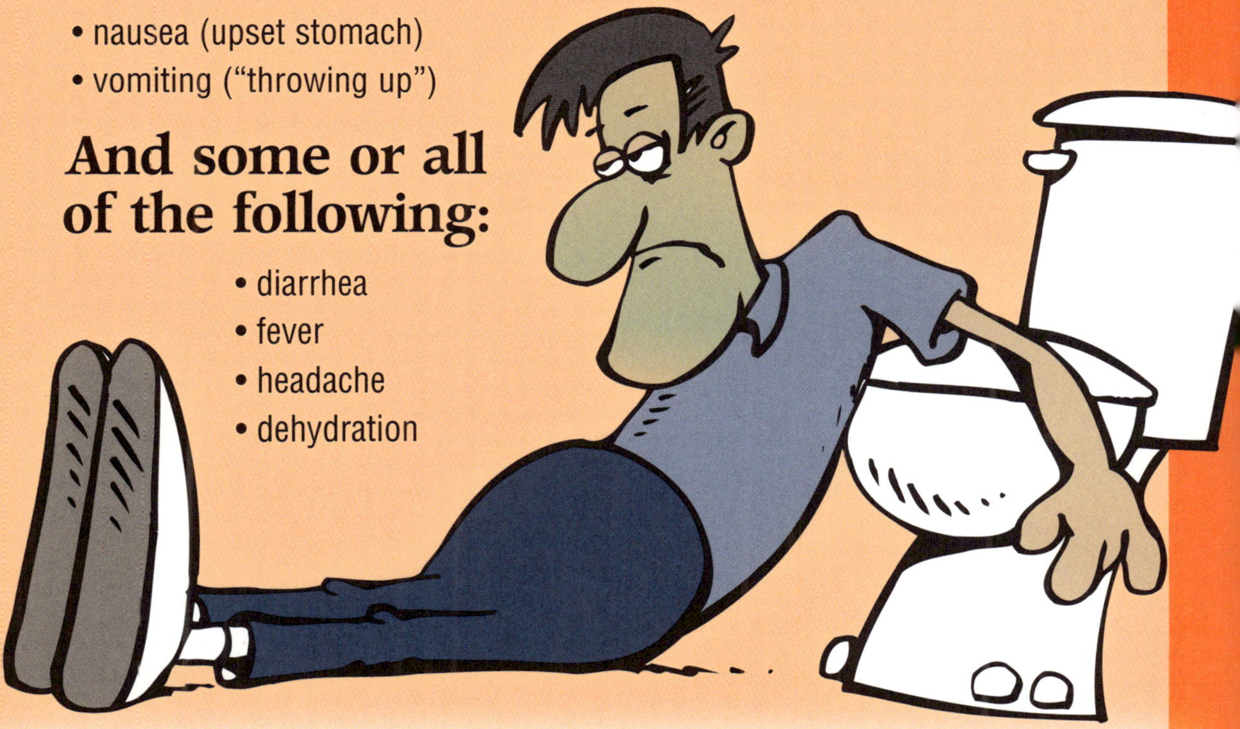

Summary:

The most common cause of nausea and vomiting (throwing up) is a viral infection usually called "the stomach flu". Most people recover from this illness within 1 or 2 days. Short-lived nausea and vomiting may also occur after eating a bacterial toxin in food; this is commonly called food poisoning. No specific treatment exists for viral infections or food poisoning of this type. Following our **Home Suggestions** will help you relieve the discomfort of this illness. Sometimes nausea and/or vomiting may be caused by medication. If you have started a new prescription medication, see your doctor. Women should check to see if they are pregnant.

Nausea, Vomiting or "Stomach Flu"
adult

START HERE

NAUSEA & VOMITING WITH OR WITHOUT DIARRHEA

↓

Are there symptoms of significant dehydration?
(See "A", page 39 for details) *or*
Have you been vomiting hourly for more than 6 hours?

YES → **GO TO YOUR DOCTOR** *or* **GO TO THE HOSPITAL NOW** (H)

NO ↓

Do you have a fever above 39.5˚C (103˚F) Rectal or 39.0˚C (102˚F) Oral? *or*
Have you been vomiting longer than 2 days? *or*
Is there blood or dark brown material in the vomit? *or*
Is there blood in your diarrhea? *or*
Do you have severe and persistant pain? *or*
Is the vomiting stopping you from taking important medication? *or*
Are you a diabetic using insulin? *or*
Have you recently hit your head hard?

YES → **GO TO YOUR DOCTOR** *or* **GO TO THE HOSPITAL NOW** (H)

NO ↓

Could you be pregnant?

NO ↓

Use HOME SUGGESTIONS

↓

Are you able to keep fluids down using the HOME SUGGESTIONS?

NO → **GO TO YOUR DOCTOR** *or* **GO TO THE HOSPITAL**

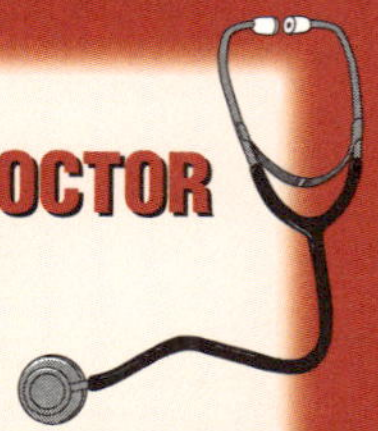

YES ↓

AFTER TWO DAYS OF RECOMMENDED TREATMENT:
Do you have ongoing symptoms?

YES → **GO TO YOUR DOCTOR** *or* **GO TO THE HOSPITAL**

NO ↓

Review this chart from the top in 6 hours

Home Suggestions

A Symptoms of dehydration:

1 You have not urinated for 8 to 10 hours.
2 You do not sweat when you are hot.
3 You have a very dry mouth and an intense thirst.
4 You feel dizzy when you stand up.
5 Confusion, fever, general weakness.

Suggestions for treating nausea and vomiting

1 Most nausea and vomiting will pass in less than 12 hours. If you rest and avoid taking anything but sips of water by mouth for a few hours, you may not need any other treatment. Severe repeated vomiting or vomiting of blood will require an immediate visit to your doctor or hospital.

2 After 8 hours it is important to begin to drink some fluid to avoid dehydration. Diarrhea causes an increase in the loss of fluid and you may need to take some medicine to help keep fluids down. See #4 on the following page for details. Using clear fluids to start is best. Water, bouillon, fruit drinks (avoiding apple or citrus fruits if diarrhea is present), flat ginger ale, or oral "rehydration" drinks, such as **Gastrolyte**, are all acceptable. Small amounts of fluid will usually stay down more easily than large amounts. Start with 1 oz, 30 mls, or 2 tablespoons every 10 minutes. **A clear fluids diet is only acceptable for 24 hours. After that period you should be using rehydration drinks**.

3 Avoid milk products during the first 24 hours of your illness. If diarrhea seems to start or increase when you drink milk, then avoid milk products until bowel movements have returned to normal. If your vomiting has stopped, then you can start to slowly introduce healthy food.

Some experts recommend starting with bland food such as toast, rice, potatoes, etc. and avoiding spicy foods and meats for a day or two. We suggest that you reintroduce food that you like in small quantities to start, but return to a full diet as your symptoms improve in 2 to 3 days.

Home Suggestions

4 You can use dimenhydrinate (**Gravol**), a non-prescription medicine to settle nausea. Ask your pharmacist for advice about this medicine. **Gravol** is safe during pregnancy. Dimenhydrinate is available in regular pills, chewable tablets, and suppositories (medication given rectally). Adults will require 50 mg every 3 to 4 hours. **Gravol** is a form of antihistamine and may cause sleepiness. Do not drive while taking **Gravol**.

5 Severe diarrhea can sometimes be controlled by using loperimide (**Imodium**). This medicine should be used only for a few days. Loperimide is especially valuable if one must go out of the home while ill. Ask your pharmacist for this medication and instructions.
Do not take loperimide if you have a high fever (39°C or 102°F taken orally) or if your stool contains blood.

6 If you are on regular medication for other health problems, then you should try to take your medicine with sips of water. If you have missed 2 or more doses, then you should seek medical advice.

7 People with diabetes requiring insulin may become very ill if they develop diarrhea or vomiting. Please go to the hospital early.

FOR A HOMEMADE REHYDRATION DRINK SEE PAGE 48.

Constipation

ADULT
Possible Symptoms:

- hard stools
- pain on passing stools
- cramping
- bloating
- gas
- hemorrhoids
- alternating constipation and diarrhea

Summary:

Different people have different bowel movement patterns. These patterns vary depending on your level of exercise, your lifestyle, and your overall general health.

Bowel activity is most influenced by how much insoluble fibre (such as wheat bran) you eat and fluids you drink. Some people will move their bowels 3 times daily, while other people may only move their bowels 3 times weekly. There is no rule that all people should move their bowels every day. Constipation usually means there has been a change to bowel movements that occur less often and that may be harder or more difficult to pass.

Constipation can be caused by some of the medication that people take. Some medications which commonly cause constipation include narcotics (codeine, morphine, etc.), aluminum containing antacids and certain high blood pressure medications.

North Americans generally eat low fibre diets. The fibre in your diet comes from the parts of plants that you cannot break down in your digestive system. There are different types of fibre. Wheat bran and coarse grains are the most effective in regulating bowel activity. Please see the **HOME SUGGESTIONS** for further advice about fibre.

Constipation
adult

START HERE

CONSTIPATION

↓

Are you using laxatives or stool softeners more than twice a week?
or
Have you noticed any bleeding?
or
Do you have ongoing pain?
or
Are you losing weight?

YES → **GO TO YOUR DOCTOR**

NO ↓

Has there been recent non-prescription or prescription medication use?

YES → Stop taking the non-prescription medication if possible. Continue the prescription medication, and Use HOME SUGGESTIONS (then go to: After 2 weeks of HOME SUGGESTIONS, are you still constipated?)

NO ↓

Use HOME SUGGESTIONS

↓

After 2 weeks of HOME SUGGESTIONS, are you still constipated?

YES → **GO TO YOUR DOCTOR**

NO ↓

Continue HOME SUGGESTIONS

Home Suggestions

1 You can use mild laxatives such as **Milk of Magnesia** at a dose of 2 tablespoons (30cc) once or twice daily. You should be careful when you use other laxatives. These usually contain a senna plant product (**Exlax**, **Correctol**, **Sennakot**, many herbal laxatives). These ingredients are harsh and can cause other bowel problems when used regularly. **Just because a product has a mild sounding name or a nicely coloured box does not mean it contains mild ingredients.** Often people only need help starting the bowels to move. This can be helped with a glycerin suppository, or **Fleet** enema. Rarely a more potent suppository is needed. **Dulcolax** suppositories can be used no more than once a week without a doctor's advice.

2 Stool softeners such as docusate sodium or docusate calcium (**Colace**, **Surfak**) may help short-term constipation that is caused by medication, pregnancy, a new illness, a change of diet or a change in life situation.

3 To improve bowel activity in the long run most people need to add more fibre to their daily diet. **The best choice is wheat bran**. The secret is to add the fibre in a slow but steady fashion.
Fibre is not a laxative. It may improve mild diarrhea as much as it may improve constipation. Start with one heaping tablespoon daily of raw wheat bran or 1/4 cup of an all-bran cereal (**All Bran**, **Bran Buds** and others). Wait at least one week between increases in your daily intake. If you tolerate the fibre increases, you can add 1 tablespoon of raw bran or 1/4 cup of all bran cereal to your daily dose each week. Aim for 2-6 tablespoons of raw bran or 1/2 to 1 cup of all bran cereal every day. Psyllium-containing products (**Metamucil**, **Prodiem Plain** and others) may also be used as fibre supplements. Remember that the slow but progressive increase in fibre will reduce the development of new symptoms or unwanted side effects.

Adding more fibre to your diet by eating more beans, fruits and raw vegetables will also improve your general health, and will make it easier to move your bowels. Be aware that not all plants contain the same kinds of fibre and may not result in the same improvement. Some will have no effect such as oat bran; others may increase gas, such as beans. Eating a higher fibre diet with reduced fat is a good idea for all people. Increasing evidence suggests that there is a reduced risk for cancer and heart disease in people who eat a higher fibre diet.

Home Suggestions

4 **The Irritable Bowel Syndrome** is a condition where a person's bowel activity is constantly changing. People with this condition often have normal or constipated bowel movements, followed by diarrhea which is accompanied by cramping pain. The symptoms of this condition may respond to the fibre advice above but if there are other symptoms that do not respond you should see your doctor. Symptoms of weight loss, rectal bleeding, or severe diarrhea should be reported to your doctor.

5 Drinking more water by itself will not make passing stools easier; however, if you are eating more fibre, then you should drink an extra one or two glasses of water per day. The increased fibre will hold the water in the stool and soften it.

6 Passing hard stool may cause you to develop hemorrhoids, or cause some bleeding from the anus. This bleeding is usually bright red and on the surface of the stool, on the paper only, or drips into the toilet. If bleeding occurs frequently, or does not improve with a softening of the stool, you should see your doctor.

Diarrhea

ADULT
Possible Symptoms:

- loose, frequent, watery bowel movements
- crampy pain
- gas
- pain around the anus
- nausea and vomiting
- bloating
- headache
- fever

Summary:

A short episode of non-bloody, loose or watery bowel movements is common for all age groups. The most common cause is a viral infection. Bacterial toxins ("food poisoning") can also cause diarrhea. Both will usually resolve on their own. The infection may be passed between family members, so wash your hands carefully and prevent the spread of the condition. Occasionally a change in diet or a new medication may cause some loose stool. If this does not improve by itself within a few days you should see your doctor. Since the diarrhea will usually resolve by itself, your self-care involves avoiding dehydration and watching for signs of more serious problems as outlined in the flowchart.

Diarrhea
adult

START HERE

DIARRHEA

Do you have nausea or vomiting?

YES → Go to "Nausea & Vomiting" page 37, then return to this page

NO

Is there blood in the stool? (Not just on the toilet paper)
or
Have you a fever above 39.5˚C (103˚F) Rectal or 39˚C (102˚F) Oral?
or
Do you have severe abdominal pain?
or
Are there signs of dehydration? (See "A", page 47)

YES → Use fever medication if required (page 6 and 78) and **GO TO YOUR DOCTOR** *or* **GO TO THE HOSPITAL NOW**

NO

Have you been taking a new medicine? (especially antibiotics)

YES → If this is a prescription medicine you should call your doctor. If this is a non-prescription medicine you should stop it and see if the diarrhea stops.

NO

Use HOME SUGGESTIONS

Have the symptoms lasted for more than 7 days without improvement?

YES → **GO TO YOUR DOCTOR**

NO

Continue HOME SUGGESTIONS

Review this chart from the top every 24 hours until your bowel movements return to normal

Home Suggestions

A Symptoms of dehydration

1 You have not urinated for 8 to 10 hours.
2 You do not sweat when you are hot.
3 You have a very dry mouth and an intense thirst.
4 You feel dizzy when you stand up.
5 Confusion, fever, general weakness.

1 It is a good idea to reduce the amount of fibre, caffeine, spicy food and alcohol in your diet for a few days until your condition improves. Otherwise, it is perfectly all right to eat your normal diet, so long as you feel well doing so. Don't eat things that seem to make the diarrhea worse, but there is no diet advice that will work for all people. It is important to drink some extra fluids. If solid food causes more diarrhea, take more fluids instead.

2 While you have diarrhea, don't eat candy or artificially sweetened foods. Drink fewer citrus juices and apple juice; these can make the diarrhea worse. Grape and pineapple juices often satisfy a taste for a fruit juice without causing more trouble. Milk products should be avoided until your condition improves. If there is an increase in the diarrhea when you start eating milk products again, then stop until the diarrhea has completely resolved.

3 A new prescription medication can have an effect on your bowels. Antibiotics are often the cause of diarrhea. Try to avoid products that contain magnesium (this includes many antacids). If you have been using a new non-prescription or over- the-counter product of any kind consider stopping it to see if this helps. Frequently a change in your stools caused by a medication only lasts a short time and will correct itself within a few days even if the medication is continued. If the diarrhea is not severe and appears to be as a result of a new medication, you might consider watching the symptom for a few days before seeing your doctor.

4 You can avoid becoming dehydrated by drinking lots of liquids such as water, fruit juices (grape or pineapple) or clear soup. Although they don't taste very good, oral "rehydration" drinks, such as **Pedialyte** or **Gastrolyte**, are very helpful in supplying the fluid and salts you need. These products can be mixed with

Home Suggestions

sugarfree **Kool-Aid** to improve their taste. In general, we suggest you start by drinking fluids that you like. If diarrhea becomes severe or prolonged we advise a switch to "rehydration" drinks.

5 Loperimide (**Imodium**) is a non-prescription or over-the-counter medication that can slow diarrhea. If you need to leave the house this can be useful. However, it will not speed your recovery. It should not be used if you see blood in the stool or if you have high fever (39°C rectal or 38.5°C oral), severe pain, nausea or vomiting.
Other medicines used for diarrhea include kaolin and pectin (**Kaopectate** and others), **Wild Strawberry** and bismuth salts, such as **Peptobismol**. Serious diarrhea will not respond to these products. **Peptobismol** should not be given to anyone under 20 years of age when they have a viral illness. See page 78 for an explanation.

6 Review other topics, such as **"FEVER"** or **"NAUSEA AND VOMITING"** if necessary.

Homemade Rehydration Drink

1 LITRE OF WATER
1/2 TEASPOON BAKING SODA
1/2 TEASPOON SALT
3-4 TABLESPOONS SUGAR
IF AVAILABLE 1/4 TABLESPOON OF "LITE SALT"
ADD UNSWEETENED DRINK CRYSTALS FOR FLAVOURING

If you are going to use a homemade rehydration drink the directions must be followed exactly.

Earache

ADULT Possible Symptoms:

- pain in or around the ear
- an itchy ear
- poor hearing
- discharge from the ear
- fever
- sore glands around the ear or in neck
- pain when the ear is tugged

Summary:

Ear infections can occur in the ear canal or behind the ear drum. Ear canal infections may develop after a day of swimming or water play (sometimes called "swimmer's ear"). The ear canal may become irritated and infected more often if you use cotton-swabs to "clean" the ear canal. Infections behind the ear drum, called "middle ear" infections, may develop during viral infections such as the cold or flu. During a cold there can be swelling and congestion which blocks the normal drainage through the Eustachian tube. **HOME SUGGESTIONS** may help in easing the discomforts of an ear infection, and help you decide when you should visit your doctor.

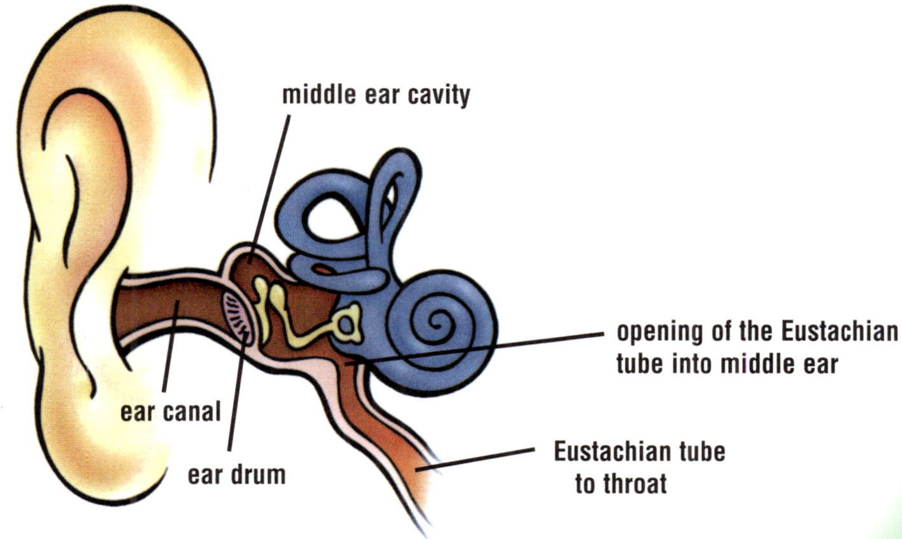

Earache
adult

START HERE

PAIN IN OR AROUND THE EAR

↓

Do you have a temperature greater than 39.5˚C (103˚F) Rectal or 39˚C (102˚F) Oral?

or

Do you have a severe headache, or severe pain on moving your neck?

or

Is there a discharge from the ear?

YES → Use fever medication if required (page 6 and 78) and **GO TO YOUR DOCTOR *or* GO TO THE HOSPITAL NOW**

NO ↓

Is the pain made worse by quick tugs or by pulling lightly on the ear lobe?

YES → **Possible ear canal infection** → Use HOME SUGGESTIONS and special SUGGESTIONS "B" (see page 52) → Is there still pain or fever after 12 to 24 hours therapy?

NO ↓

Possible middle ear infection

Use HOME SUGGESTIONS and special SUGGESTIONS "A" (see page 51)

↓

Is there still pain or fever after 12 to 24 hours therapy?

YES → **GO TO YOUR DOCTOR *or* GO TO THE HOSPITAL**

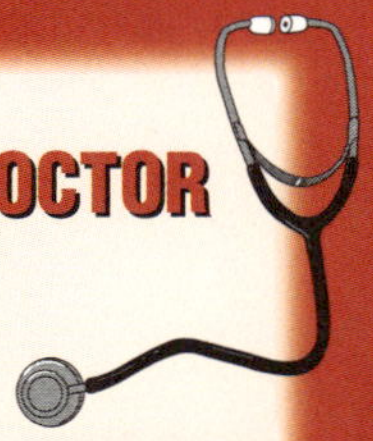

NO ↓

Continue HOME SUGGESTIONS for one week

Home Suggestions

*If you have a fever, please see the "**FEVER**" section on pages 3-6.*

1 Most people are very anxious to control the pain caused by middle ear infections. Use acetaminophen (**Tylenol** and others), ASA (**Aspirin** and others) or Ibuprofen (**Advil**, **Motrin** and others). See page 78 for pain medication use. See page 6 for acetaminophen dosage.
If there is no improvement in the pain or condition within 24-36 hours, it may be necessary to take a course of antibiotics. Antibiotics do not relieve pain immediately. We recommend treating yourself with pain medication early and seeking advice about antibiotics during the light of day.

2 Put a warm cloth on the ear for 20 minutes several times daily. This will often help relieve pain.

3 Warm oil drops in the ear canal may give some relief from pain. One can use **Auralgan** drops or use mineral oil, cooking oil or olive oil. Touch your skin with the oil to test how hot it is before putting it in your ear canal.

Special suggestions "A"

For middle ear infections:

1 You can sometimes help relieve discomfort by treating the early symptoms of nasal congestion and ear fullness with decongestants. These agents may help middle ear draining. See page 74 for further information about decongestants. People with severe heart disease, poorly controlled high blood pressure or severe asthma should not use decongestant medications.

2 Try to "pop" your ears by blowing gently with your mouth closed and your nose pinched. Do this several times daily.

Home Suggestions

Special suggestions "B"

For ear canal infections ("Swimmer's Ear"):

1 Do not get water in your ear for 7 days, if possible. If you do, shake your head to remove it. You can also use a blow dryer on low setting, held 6 to 12 inches from the ear, to dry the ear canal. A few drops of a drying agent will help the ear dry faster. **Burosol** or a mixture of 1 tablespoon vinegar and 1 tablespoon of warm water make good drying agents. Put these drops right into the ear canal.

2 This is an infection which may respond to non-prescription antibiotic drops (**Polysporin**). Use 2 drops 4 times daily.

3 **DO NOT TRY TO CLEAN OUT THE EAR WITH A COTTON SWAB.** This may increase your risk of ear infections.

4 You may want to prevent another ear canal infection. Placing a couple of drops of an antibiotic solution (**Polysporin**) in the ear after a day of swimming or putting a couple of drops of cooking oil, olive oil or mineral oil in the ear canal before swimming may prevent repeat infections. Ear plugs designed to prevent water from getting in the ear canal may also be helpful. You should not use hard plastic ear plugs.

Conjunctivitis or "Pink Eye"

Possible Symptoms:

Affecting one or both eyes

- red eyes
- swollen lids
- itchiness
- crusting or pussy eyes
- gritty eyes
- increased tearing

Summary:

"Pink Eye" is an irritation of the white of the eye and the eyelid. It can make your eye look red or pinkish in colour. It is easily passed from person to person. Thorough handwashing by both the sufferer and the caretaker is very important to prevent the spread of infection.

Often when someone is suffering from "Pink Eye" the eyes will make more tears. This can make the eyes uncomfortable and crusty after sleep. Clean the crusts away by holding a warm, damp cloth gently over the eye. Recheck the eye about an hour later. If there is just a small quantity of crusty discharge, then the cause of this eye irritation is likely viral. If, however, a creamy, runny or stringy discharge is forming then the cause is probably bacterial. Conjunctivitis is irritating but should not be too painful. If there is a lot of pain, you should see your doctor. Follow the instructions in **Home Suggestions** and you should be able to take care of this illness at home.

Please note: During the allergy season (spring through fall), a very itchy eye most likely indicates an allergic reaction rather than "Pink Eye".

Conjunctivitis or "Pink Eye"

START HERE

PINK EYE

Is there severe redness or swelling around the eye?
or
Is there pain around or behind the eye or is there pain with eye movements?
or
Is there a fever present? (see page 3)
or
Are you having trouble seeing?
or
Is this a newborn child?
or
Has there been recent eye surgery?
or
Do you wear contact lenses?
or
Does bright light hurt the eyes?
or
Have you noticed the pupils are different sizes?

YES → Use acetaminophen, ibuprofen, or ASA for pain (see page 78) and then **GO TO YOUR DOCTOR** *or* **GO TO THE HOSPITAL NOW**

NO ↓

60 minutes after cleaning your eyes with warm water and a cloth, is there (choose one)...

A creamy discharge from the eye? → **Use HOME SUGGESTIONS "A" Page 55**

A crusty discharge from the eye? → **Use HOME SUGGESTIONS "B" Page 55**

Start again from the top of this chart every 6-8 hours

If not better within 48-72 hours → **GO TO YOUR DOCTOR**

Home Suggestions

Suggestions "A"

1 Try a non-prescription antibiotic drop such as **Polysporin**. Place 2 drops in the "pink" eye four times daily. Continue this treatment for 7 days. If the eye is not improving after 3 days you should see your doctor.

2 Clean the eye with a warm cloth as necessary.

3 Warm or cool cloths put on the eye for 20 minutes at a time may soothe the discomfort, pressure and swelling. Use whatever seems to work the best for you.

4 Avoid smoke and other things which bother your eyes.

5 Avoid wearing contact lenses until your eye has been normal for 2-3 days.

Suggestions "B"

1 Non-prescription decongestant eye drops, such as **Visine** or **Vasocon**, can help soothe the eye. Those with severe heart disease or poorly controlled blood pressure should avoid decongestant medications. See page 74 for more details about decongestant medications. Ask your pharmacist for help in choosing these medications.

2 Clean the eye with a warm cloth as necessary.

3 Avoid smoke and other things which bother your eyes.

4 If there is severe itching, there may be an allergy causing the problem. Antihistamine pills or antihistamine containing eye drops may help. See page 75 for more details about antihistamines. Ask your pharmacist for help in selecting these medicines.

5 Avoid wearing contact lenses until your eye has been normal for 2-3 days.

Heartburn

Possible Symptoms:

- burning discomfort behind the breastbone (increased by bending over, lying down and eating)
- regurgitation of food and a sour taste in the mouth (especially on bending over)
- associated symptoms may include bloating after meals

Summary:

Heartburn is a burning discomfort felt behind the breastbone. This discomfort is made worse by meals, bending over, or lying down. Fatty foods, spicy foods, peppermint, coffee, alcohol and cigarette smoking may also cause heartburn. Almost 90% of the population will get heartburn from time to time. Many people, however, will have episodes of heartburn more often. Those who suffer from severe or frequent heartburn may need regular medication to control symptoms. Anyone who has heartburn and difficulty swallowing should see their doctor. Sometimes heartburn can be increased by prescription medicines. If you have started a new medicine and have been suffering with heartburn, please see your doctor. Use the flowchart to help you decide if you should see your doctor.

Heartburn

START HERE

HEARTBURN

Is there any sweating, vomiting, shortness of breath, dizziness or chest tightness?
or
Have you passed bloody or thick black bowel movements?
or
Have you vomited blood?

YES → **GO TO THE HOSPITAL NOW** (H)

NO ↓

Try an antacid, see HOME SUGGESTIONS

Has the severe or new heartburn continued for over 10 minutes after a dose of antacid?

YES → **GO TO THE HOSPITAL NOW** (H)

NO ↓

Have you had unexpected weight loss?
or
Does food stick on the way down after swallowing?
or
Do you have heartburn more than 3 times per week?

YES → Use HOME SUGGESTIONS and **GO TO YOUR DOCTOR**

NO ↓

Use HOME SUGGESTIONS

Do you still have symptoms after 2 to 4 weeks of treatment?

YES → **GO TO YOUR DOCTOR**

NO ↓

Continue therapy.

Home Suggestions

1 Antacids are non-prescription (over the counter) products, which neutralize acid. They are available in liquid and tablet form. They may contain magnesium hydroxide (which may cause diarrhea), aluminum hydroxide (which may cause constipation) or calcium carbonate (**Tums**, **Rolaids** and others). Antacids may contain a mixture of magnesium and aluminum (**Maalox** or **Riopan** for example) to reduce any side effects. You can take antacids when you want rapid relief of heartburn.
There will not be any long lasting effect. If taken regularly after meals or at bedtime then they may help prevent or reduce your heartburn discomfort. If you need to take antacids more than twice a day then you should see your doctor.

2 Medicines containing alginic acid, such as **Gaviscon**, may prevent heartburn symptoms when taken after meals or at bedtime. This medicine is not a true antacid, but creates a barrier which prevents the acid from coming back up from your stomach.

3 You can help yourself feel better by making some changes to your daily habits:
- do not lie down for 2 hours after meals
- do not eat within 2 hours of bedtime
- raise or elevate the head of your bed 6 inches on blocks. Propping yourself with pillows won't be as helpful and may actually cause more trouble.
- cut back or eliminate your caffeine intake. Caffeine is found in coffee, tea, chocolate and most cola drinks
- cut back or eliminate your use of alcohol and cigarettes
- cut back your use of ASA and anti-inflammatory medication if possible. Try acetaminophen (**Tylenol** and others) instead.
- cut back your intake of fatty foods you eat: high fat meats, fried foods, gravy and sauces
- spicy foods and peppermint often cause heartburn
- if a food causes you discomfort, avoid eating it a second time

4 Some medications may increase heartburn symptoms. If you develop new symptoms after starting a new medication consult your doctor.

5 Also available without a prescription are the acid-reducing drugs cimetidine (**Tagamet**), ranitidine (**Zantac**), famotidine (**Pepcid**) and nizatidine (**Axid**). These medications are also available in higher strengths as prescription medications. If you try one of these medications and find that it does not give you complete relief of symptoms or that you require regular or prolonged use of these drugs to feel well you should discuss this with your doctor.

Bee Stings or Insect Bites

Possible Symptoms:

minor and localized

- pain
- redness
- swelling

major or severe (anaphylaxis)

- shortness of breath
- swelling of the mouth, tongue, or throat
- lightheadedness or dizziness
- severe rash over large areas

Summary:

Most insect bites and stings cause reactions at the site of the bite or sting. The discomfort of these bites is usually easy to relieve and treat at home. The use of cold compresses and antihistamines will help significantly.

Bee Stings or Insect Bites

START HERE

BEE STINGS OR INSECT BITES
You have been bitten or stung by an insect (bee, wasp, hornet, mosquito, blackfly, etc.).

Do you have difficulty breathing?
or
Do you have mouth or throat swelling?
or
Are you severely lightheaded or dizzy?
or
Do you have a history of a previous severe reaction to insect bites or stings?

YES → If available: Use adrenalin kit and take supplied antihistamine pill. Then **GO TO THE HOSPITAL NOW**

NO ↓

Are there a large number of stings? (more than 10 stings from bees, hornets, wasps etc.)

YES → **GO TO YOUR DOCTOR *or* GO TO THE HOSPITAL NOW**

NO ↓

Use HOME SUGGESTIONS

↓

AFTER 48 HOURS:
Is there a fever, increasing redness or red streaking up a limb?

YES → **GO TO YOUR DOCTOR *or* GO TO THE HOSPITAL**

NO ↓

Use HOME SUGGESTIONS

↓

If any symptoms develop after 7 to 10 days

YES → **GO TO YOUR DOCTOR**

Home Suggestions

1 If you have previously had an allergic reaction to a sting or bite, you should immediately take an antihistamine (see page 75). If you do not have a known allergy you should wait for redness, swelling or itching to develop and take an antihistamine to relieve these symptoms if they occur.

2 Apply a cold pack immediately for a maximum of 20 minutes; this will reduce the redness and swelling. You can reapply this cold pack for 20 minutes every hour as long as there is redness and swelling.

3 In relieving the discomfort of a sting, it is important to make sure you have removed the stinger. At the end of the stinger there is a venom sack which can continue to release venom as long as it is embedded in the skin. To remove the stinger you should gently scrape it out from the side with a sharp-edged object like a knife. ***Do not squeeze and pull***.

4 Non-prescription or over-the-counter antihistamine or hydrocortisone cream can help reduce the skin irritation and itch. Ask your pharmacist to help you choose this medicine.

5 If you have had a serious reaction in the past, you should carry an adrenalin kit with you. Discuss this with your doctor.

Strains and Sprains of the Limbs

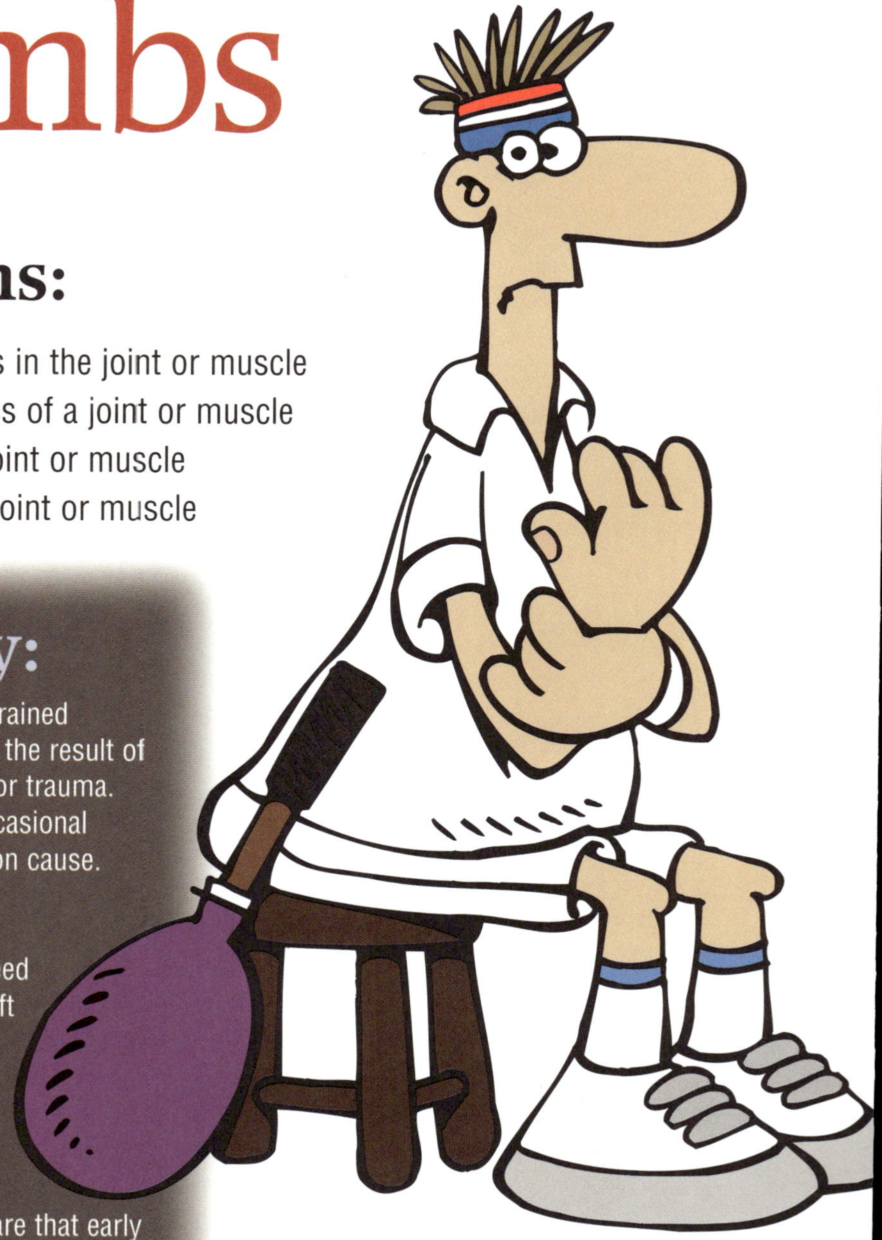

Possible Symptoms:

- pain and tenderness in the joint or muscle
- swelling and redness of a joint or muscle
- bruising around a joint or muscle
- difficulty moving a joint or muscle

Summary:

Strained muscles and sprained ligaments are commonly the result of overuse, sports activity, or trauma. Playing a sport on an occasional basis is the most common cause. Using R.I.C.E.: Rest, Ice, Compression, Elevation immediately will help speed your recovery. These "soft tissue" injuries should slowly improve over a period of 1 week. Returning to regular activity too early may prolong an injury. Be aware that early in the day may be one of the most difficult times due to the stiffness that can develop as a result of being inactive throughout the night. Give yourself time to improve over the morning hours.

Strains and Sprains of the Limbs

START HERE

POSSIBLE LIGAMENT SPRAIN OR MUSCLE STRAIN

↓

You cannot stand on your injured leg?
or
You cannot bend your joint normally?
or
Is there obvious deformity of the joint or limb?
or
Is the skin cut or scraped over the area?

YES → Use pain medication (acetaminophen, ASA, ibuprofen, etc.) and **GO TO YOUR DOCTOR** *or* **GO TO THE HOSPITAL NOW**

NO ↓

Use HOME SUGGESTIONS

↓

Is the pain still bad after using HOME SUGGESTIONS?

YES → **GO TO YOUR DOCTOR** *or* **GO TO THE HOSPITAL**

↓

OVER THE FIRST 48 HOURS
Is there increasing swelling or redness despite treatment?
or
Is it remaining difficult to move the joint?
or
Is there continued severe pain?

YES → **GO TO YOUR DOCTOR** *or* **GO TO THE HOSPITAL**

NO ↓

Continue HOME SUGGESTIONS

↓

Is the muscle or joint function still abnormal or is there significant pain after 1 week?

YES → **GO TO YOUR DOCTOR**

Home Suggestions

1 R.I.C.E. REST, ICE, COMPRESSION, ELEVATION

Rest the area for the first 48 hours. After this time your body will let you know how much you should be doing. Using a sling or crutches may be helpful.

Ice is used to reduce swelling. Use ice, cold packs, or even frozen peas or corn for proper shaping to your injured area. Start by applying the ice for 20 minutes on, 20 minutes off, for the first 2 hours. Thereafter, use ice 5 times daily for the first 2 days. Protect your bare skin from very cold objects to prevent frostbite. Put ice in a towel.

Use an elastic bandage to wrap areas of swelling. You can also use these type of bandages for support.

Elevation of a limb will help reduce swelling. Place your arm in a sling or elevate your foot or leg on a pillow.

2 After the first 48 hours, you can continue with ice or switch to heat therapy. Use whatever makes you feel better. You may find that alternating between cold and hot therapy feels good. You should not use heat during the first 48 hours for it may increase swelling. Remember to protect bare skin from hot water bottles etc. to prevent burns. Put the hot water bottles in a towel.

3 After 48 hours begin to move the injured area but avoid anything causing serious pain.

Scrapes and Abrasions

Possible Symptoms:

- scraped skin that may or may not bleed
- dirt in the abrasion
- not a cut, the skin is not spread apart

Summary:

Scrapes and abrasions are very common and easily treated at home. If the area affected is large, deeply injured or appears infected you should see a doctor. Treatment depends on good initial cleaning and watching for infection. Most scrapes or abrasions will heal in 1-2 weeks.

Scrapes and Abrasions

START HERE

SCRAPE OR ABRASION INJURY

↓

Does the abrasion go deeper than the skin layer? → **YES** → **GO TO YOUR DOCTOR *or* GO TO THE HOSPITAL**

↓ **NO**

Use HOME SUGGESTIONS

↓

Is there dirt you cannot remove?

or

Is there increased redness around the abrasion?

or

Is there red streaking up the limb?

or

Is there pus coming from the area?

or

Is there increasing pain?

or

Have you got a fever? (see pages 3-6)

→ **YES** → **GO TO YOUR DOCTOR *or* GO TO THE HOSPITAL**

↓ **NO**

Continue HOME SUGGESTIONS

Review the abrasion daily

Home Suggestions

1 Wash the abrasion with warm water. Letting water run over the area is best. If discomfort prevents you from doing this, then soak the scraped area with warm wet cloths. You may need to scrub the area to remove dirt. You may repeat the washing as many times as necessary to clean the scraped area thoroughly. Clean water and soap are all you really need to do this.

2 If pain prevents cleaning all the material out of the abrasion, you should use a local anaesthetic like **Bactine** to make the process less painful.

3 Take acetaminophin (**Tylenol** and others), ASA (**Aspirin** and others) or ibuprofen (**Advil**, **Motrin**, and others) for pain. Do not give ASA to anyone under 20 years of age. See page 78 for details.

4 We suggest you apply an antibiotic ointment (**Polysporin** and others) 2 or 3 times daily and cover the abrasion with a bandage, gauze or non-stick **Telfa**. Use enough ointment to prevent the bandage from sticking to the injured skin. Covering the abrasion may speed healing and keep the area clean.

5 You should check that a tetanus booster immunization has been received within the last 10 years. If not you should see your doctor. The last regularly scheduled immunization is usually at age 14.

Minor Burns

Possible Symptoms:

- redness
- tenderness
- pain
- swelling
- blistering

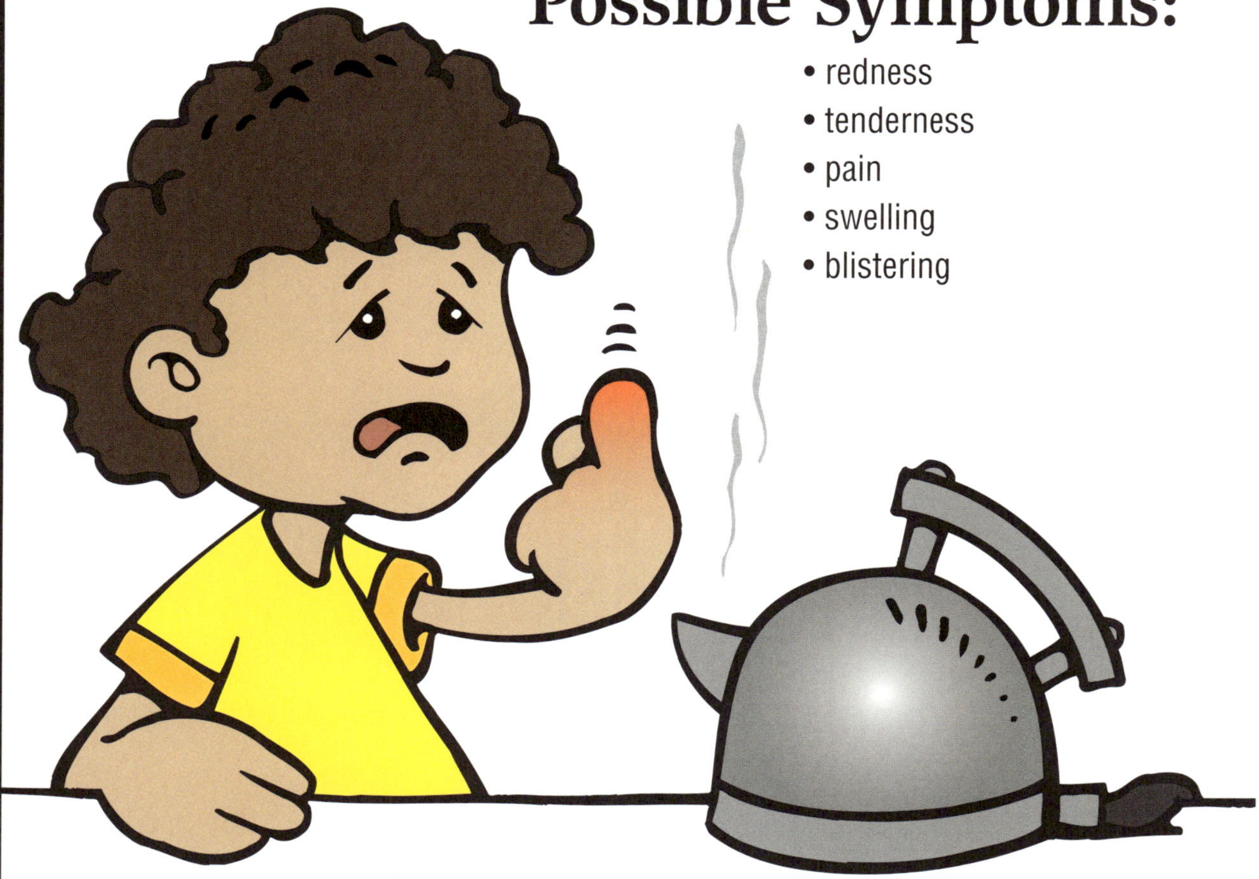

Summary:

Small burns, even if blistered can be treated at home. Burns must be cleaned and kept clean. Using simple soap and warm water is all that is needed. It is important to reassess your burn as it can change over time. Minor burns should heal within 1-2 weeks.

Minor Burns

START HERE

BURN

↓

Is the burn large?
or
Is the burn on the face?
or
Is the burn in the groin area?
or
Is there a large blister?
or
Is the skin broken?
or
Is the skin white and painless?

YES → Use HOME SUGGESTIONS and **GO TO THE HOSPITAL NOW**

NO ↓

Use HOME SUGGESTIONS

Is the pain controlled with HOME SUGGESTIONS?
or
Is there spreading redness around the burn?
or
Is there red streaking going up the limb?
or
Is there a fever now? (see pages 3-6)

YES → **GO TO YOUR DOCTOR *or* GO TO THE HOSPITAL**

NO ↓

Continue HOME SUGGESTIONS

Review the burn daily

Home Suggestions

1 Immediately place the burned area into cold water or apply a cold compress for 10-15 minutes. This will cool the hot skin and reduce further injury.

2 Burned skin must be kept clean. Wash it with soap and water. Putting some local anaesthetic like **Bactine** or benzocaine (**Solarcaine**) on the burn may allow you to clean and dress the burn with less pain.

3 If a blister breaks, apply an antibiotic ointment (**Polysporin** and others) and cover with a bandage, gauze or non-stick **Telfa**. Apply enough ointment to prevent the bandage from sticking to the injured skin.

4 If the skin is unbroken, you can apply a moisturizing skin cream 3 times daily. Some of these may contain aloe, a natural healing substance.

5 If a burned area is throbbing you may feel better if you elevate it. Place your arm in a sling or your foot on a pillow.

6 If you do not have stomach problems, you could use an anti-inflammatory pain medication like ASA (**Aspirin** and others) or ibuprofen (**Advil**, **Motrin**, and others). See page 78 for more details. Do not use ASA (**Aspirin** and others) in anyone under 20 years of age.

Sunburn

Possible Symptoms:

- red tender skin
- blistered skin
- fever or chills
- dehydration (see "A" page 25 for children or page 47 for adults)
- flaking, itching, tingling skin
- sunstroke (page 73)

Summary:

Sunburns are similar to other burns caused by hot objects. Sunburns usually cover larger areas of skin but are usually minor burns. They are commonly associated with chills, fever and possibly dehydration. Treatment of a burn includes cooling the skin, controlling the discomfort and protecting the skin from further injury. Watch for dehydration (sunstroke). Burning and tanning both increase your risk of skin cancer. There is no such thing as a good burn. Please remember to put sunscreen on. Be sure to put sunscreen on children even if they are going out for only short periods of time. It usually takes only 20-30 minutes to burn in the summer.

Sunburn

START HERE

SUNBURN

↓

Do you have a temperature greater than 39˚C (102˚F) Rectal or 38.5˚C (101˚F) Oral?

or

Is there severe blistering?

or

Do you have symptoms of sunstroke?
(see "A" page 73)

YES → Use pain medication (acetaminophen, ASA, ibuprofen, etc.) *and* **GO TO THE HOSPITAL NOW**

NO ↓

Use HOME SUGGESTIONS

Continue to reassess temperature and symptoms during the next 12 hours

↓

Are you getting sicker?

YES → **GO TO YOUR DOCTOR *or* GO TO THE HOSPITAL**

NO ↓

Continue HOME SUGGESTIONS

Home Suggestions

Ⓐ Symptoms of dehydration and sunstroke

1 temperature greater 39°C (102°F) rectal or 38.5°C (101°F) oral
2 heart rate greater than 100 beats per minute at rest
3 no sweating
4 light headedness when you stand
5 confusion
6 muscle cramps
7 passing out
8 headache
9 nausea and vomiting

All of the above symptoms may develop more easily when the victim has been drinking alcohol.

Therapy for Sunburn

1 Cool the burned skin with a cold bath, damp towel or cold shower.

2 Drink plenty of non-alcoholic fluids.

3 Apply a moisturizing cream to the burned area liberally, several times daily.

4 Use acetaminophen (**Tylenol** and others), ASA (**Aspirin** and others) or ibuprofen (**Advil**, **Motrin** and others) for pain and fever control. Do not give ASA to those under 20 years of age. See page 78 for details.

5 Painful skin may be treated with local anaesthetic spray or ointments such as benzocaine (**Solarcaine**).

6 Stinging or itching can be treated with 0.5% hydrocortisone available without a prescription.

7 Antihistamines may reduce itching. See page 75 for details.

8 Don't expose burned skin to the sun even with sunscreen applied. Wear a hat, long sleeves and long pants.

9 Always wear a hat and apply a sunblock 30 or higher to prevent sunburn. Apply sunblock liberally to children.

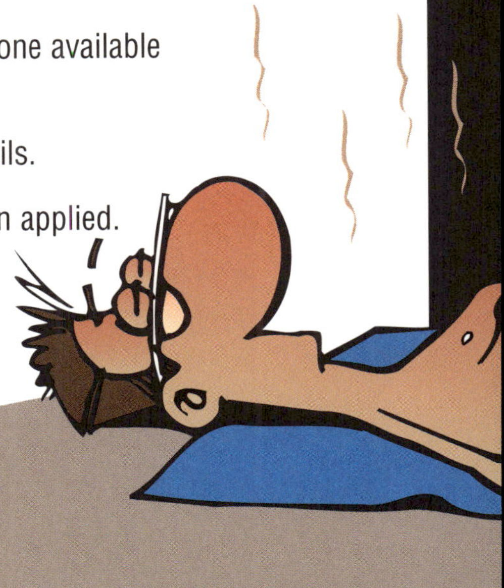

information

All about decongestants

Decongestants are medicines which reduce the swelling and dry up the lining of the nasal passages. These medicines are usually taken as a tablet by mouth or as a nasal spray. Decongestants have difficult to remember names such as ephedrine, phenylephrine, phenylpropanolamine, and pseudoephedrine, and sprays may contain xylometazoline, or oxymetazoline. Many of these drugs are similar to adrenaline, a natural substance produced by your body. These medicines may be dangerous for people with serious heart disease or poorly controlled high blood pressure. They can speed up the heart rate and increase blood pressure. Those suffering with asthma should use these medications with caution.

Decongestants are frequently combined with an antihistamine and pain or fever medication like acetaminophen or ibuprofen. Decongestant medicines, when you are able to take them, can be very helpful in relieving some of the symptoms of a cold or sinus congestion. They may also reduce the runny nose of an allergic reaction, but will not stop the allergic reaction as an antihistamine can. Routine use of nasal sprays may actually result in an increased runny nose. Nasal sprays should not be used on a regular or prolonged basis. We recommend use for only 3 days at the most.

Some people will have extremely uncomfortable eyes during allergic reactions. There are eye drop medications which contain decongestants (naphazoline, xylometazoline) which will help reduce redness. They may also contain weak antihistamines (antazoline or pheniramine). Commonly purchased products include **Visine** and **Vasocon**.

Adults will find that some trial and error may be necessary to find a decongestant, an antihistamine, or combination medications which will give them good relief from cold or allergy symptoms without causing unwanted side effects. Remember that combination medications, despite the fact they try to be all things to all people, may not be your best choice for all cold symptoms or allergic reactions. Some people will be better off using a pure antihistamine or decongestant medication.

information

We find that children benefit most from cold medications taken at night. Frequently children do not need medicine during the day. The combination of a sedating antihistamine with a decongestant may therefore be useful when taken at night. We suggest a combination medicine like **Dimetapp**.

We recommend that pain medication be taken in pure form and given in the appropriate dose for weight (see page 6).

For children under two years of age we, recommend infant preparations. These are more concentrated and therefore require less volume to get a proper dose. Read the label carefully and ask your Pharmacist for advice. Watch all children for the development of unwanted hyperactivity with antihistamines. If this does occur, you can buy products which contain only a decongestant.

TAKE THIS BOOK WITH YOU WHEN YOU GO SHOPPING FOR COLD OR ALLERGY MEDICATION.

All about antihistamines

The way you feel when you have a cold can be similar to the way you feel when you are suffering with allergies. The stuffy nose and runny red eyes caused by allergies can feel the same as a cold, but they are different. Many non-prescription medicines available at your drug store combine drugs aimed at both colds and allergies in order to be all things to all people. Often these medicines are combined in such a way which gives you lower doses of these medicines than if you were buying them separately. You can, however, buy non-prescription or over-the-counter medicines which are either purely decongestants or antihistamines.

Different people respond in different ways to certain medications or combinations of medications. This may depend upon the cause of your problem, but also upon how each of us reacts to a particular medicine. Some people will find that a certain cold or allergy medication works better for them; as a result, finding the right medicine for you may require some trial and error.

information

Medicine packaging doesn't always tell you whether the ingredients are antihistamines or decongestants. Instead they give you the chemical names which are difficult to pronounce or remember. Do not be afraid to ask your pharmacist for help; he/she can be a helpful source of information. Also, use this page, and the information below, to help you when you are shopping for cold or allergy medicine.

Antihistamines are medications which reduce the effect of histamine. Histamine is what causes the runny, red, and itchy eyes, runny nose, swollen throat and rashes of allergies. If you take an antihistamine early in your allergic response you can make your reaction less severe. If you take the antihistamine before the reaction starts, you may avoid the allergic reaction altogether. Almost all antihistamines are available without a prescription. Please ask your pharmacist. An eye drop commonly used to prevent allergic reactions is **Opticrom**.

Antihistamines can be divided into two main groups:

1) those which can make you sleepy (sedating), and

2) those which do not make you sleepy (non-sedating). The first group may well give you a stronger antihistamine effect in an emergency and may work well for skin reactions. These are also helpful when sleeping. (In fact most over-the-counter sleeping pills contain antihistamines as their main ingredient.) Antihistamines are sold in many forms: tablets, nasal spray, eyedrops and lotions. Some will last all day; others have to be taken as often as every 4 hours. The shorter acting medications may be more useful for emergency use. Diphenhydramine (**Benadryl**) is the drug of first choice of many doctors for severe allergic reactions.

The antihistamines which may cause sedation include diphenhydramine (**Benadryl**), brompheniramine (**Dimetane**), chlorpheniramine (**Chlortripolon**), and clemastine (**Tavist**) to name only a few. They are also available in combination medications, usually with a decongestant and sometimes with something to reduce a cough. They also come with pain and fever medicines like acetaminophen and ibuprofen. In combination with other cold therapy, an antihistamine can help give you a much needed sleep. A word of caution: some people may have an opposite reaction and experience an increase in activity and alertness. Children may be described as becoming "hyper". This can happen with any antihistamine.

The non-sedating ("no sleepiness") antihistamine group includes: astemizole (**Hismanal**), loratadine (**Claritin**), and fexofenadine (**Allegra**) These non-sedating antihistamines are better choices for regular daily use during the allergy season. They help prevent symptoms without making you sleepy. Astemizole may take up to 3 or 4 days to work when taken regularly. Loratadine and terfenadine will work faster. Astemizole (**Hismanal**) have been found to have **potentially serious side effects** if taken with the antibiotics erythromycin or clarithromycin (**Biaxin**), the antifungal preparation ketoconazole, or the stomach medication cisapride (**Prepulsid**).

How and when to use antibiotics

Infections often result from an exposure to bacteria, viruses or parasites. Many common health problems develop from viral infections. These include the common cold, the flu and gastroenteritis. There is no specific therapy for viral infections and they usually clear up after a few days without any special therapy.

Antibiotics are drugs which are useful in treating people with bacterial infections. Bacterial infections are commonly found in the lung, urine, sinuses, throat, ears and skin. Antibiotics can help slow down or stop the growth of bacteria so that the body's own defences can fight the infection. When you are given a prescription for an antibiotic, you will notice that it is given for a certain number of days. It is very important to take the entire prescription as instructed on the label. If you only take the medicine for a couple of days and the infection is not completely cleared, it can come back and cause more trouble.

Antibiotics may not kill all bacteria. Some attack a specific kind of bacteria, while others may be able to kill a larger group of bacteria. Your doctor tries to choose an antibiotic medicine which is specific to the bacteria causing your illness. In this way the medicine is not helping to make other bacteria resistant or immune to the drug's effects. For this reason, it is very important to take antibiotics only when we really need them. The flow charts in this book will help you decide when your illness requires a doctor's attention and possible antibiotic therapy.

Antibiotics can often cause stomach upset or bowel changes. Diarrhea is the most common side effect of these medicines. If your diarrhea is severe or contains blood, you should contact your doctor or go to the hospital.

Another caution: Some antibiotics can become toxic (poisonous) or weakened if stored for a long time. Unfinished or old medications should be thrown out. If you have a large quantity to throw out, your pharmacist can help. Never give a medicine prescribed for you to someone else.

All about pain and fever medications

Most people are familiar with **Aspirin** and **Tylenol**. These are the brand names of the very common medications ASA (acetylsalicylic acid) and acetaminophen. These medications are used to treat pain and fever. ASA, but not acetaminophen, can also relieve inflammation (swelling, heat, or redness).

One of the new medications you can buy at your pharmacy without a prescription is ibuprofen (**Advil**, **Motrin** and others). This medication belongs to the same family of medications to which ASA belongs. These are Nonsteroidal Anti-Inflammatory Drugs or, as they are sometimes called, NSAIDs. These medicines can relieve pain, lower a fever, and also reduce inflammation. You might think that these medicines are the best overall for they can be used for both pain and inflammation. Unfortunately they can cause stomach ulcers and kidney problems in some people. Sometimes they upset your stomach if not taken with food.

information

ASA should not be given to people under the age of 20 when they have a viral illness. There is a liver disease called Reye's Syndrome which may be caused by taking ASA during influenza infections and the chicken pox. ASA, which stands for acetylsalicylic acid, is from a drug group called salicylates. Another member of this group of medicines is bismuth subsalicylate (**Peptobismol**). We recommend that you do not give these medicines to those under 20 years of age.

Ibuprofen (**Advil**, **Motrin** and others), a NSAID as described above, does not carry the same risk of causing Reye's Syndrome. It can be used alone or occasionally along with acetaminophen in those whose pain and fever do not respond well to acetominophen. Ibuprofen may also relieve discomfort for a longer time (6 to 8 hours versus 4 to 6 hours for acetaminophen). Ibuprofen is also sold in children's strength. Acetaminophen remains the first choice for pain and fever in children. We feel acetaminophen has the best overall safety profile.

You may have heard people say that one or another of these medications works better for their pain. Although this may have been the case, often the problem in controlling pain is that the appropriate dose of the medicine has not been taken. This is especially true in treating children's illnesses. The instructions on the package usually suggest dosages based on age and as a result only the lightest people in an age group get the right dose. You can manage pain better if you take the correct dosage based on your weight. We have created an acetaminophen dosage schedule to make this easier (see page 6). Adults require between 600 and 1000 mg of acetaminophen every 4 hours to relieve pain.

Regular acetaminophen tablets contain 325mg and the extra strength tablets contain 500mg. Serious pain will require 2 to 3 regular tablets or 2 extra strength tablets. You should look carefully at the bottles and price them by the number of effective doses available in the bottle. Ibuprofen dosage should be individualized at 10mg per kg body weight every 6 to 8 hours. Adults can take up to 800mg every 8 hours, but should use the lowest dose that is effective.

information

There are several pain medications which add caffeine to ASA. This combination can help to improve the effectiveness of the ASA, but it is not necessary in most situations. The caffeine content is equivalent to about a half cup of coffee.

Sometimes a narcotic-type medication is added to ASA or acetaminophen to improve the pain-relieving effect. Usually codeine is added. Adding 8 mg of codeine to the regular tablets produces a medicine which is stronger but still available without a prescription. You will have to ask your pharmacist for this type of medication.

REMEMBER: When you are using a medicine for relieving pain or for controlling a fever, you will be most successful if you give the medicine at regular intervals. If you wait until the pain is really bad or until the fever has crept really high again, it will take longer to get it under control.

See page 6 for acetaminophen dosage.

information

The most important person on your health care team is you

No one knows you better than you do. You know all about yourself, from your symptoms to your lifestyle and habits. No one can make changes without you. You are the one in control and ultimately carry much of the responsibility. Good health and fitness cannot be attained without you being an active participant.

Personal principles

1 *Know your goals.* To improve the health care that you receive you should try to define your goals. To some people, good health means that they have achieved the goal of avoiding diagnosis and treatment for any medical conditions. To others the goal is to function in life at the highest level possible and they will do whatever is necessary to achieve this goal. To some, the only real goal is to live a long life.

2 *Know your comfort range.* People differ greatly on how active they wish to become in the decision making process involving their personal health care. The ideal relationship with your physician is an open partnership. We believe that this has definite advantages and allows you the most involvement, however, many people are not comfortable in this role. There are those who want to say to their physician "Just tell me what you think is best." We believe that you have the right to exist in your comfort zone. No single solution is right for everyone.

3 *Don't expect your physician to be a "Jack of all trades."* While your physician may be familiar with many forms of medicine, it is likely due to his/her personal interests. A medical doctor has been trained in specific areas and in certain methods. The healthcare industry is wide and varied and your physician is not an expert in all forms of health care. He/she is likely to be the best coordinator of your care and you should keep him/her informed.

4 *Unfortunately there are no guarantees in health.* It is a reality of life that some people take very good care of themselves and yet are never really "healthy." On the other hand some people are quite abusive to their bodies but their health never seems to show the effects of their behavior. While it seems unfair, we can't always link our lifestyle to our health condition. A healthy lifestyle certainly increases our chances of being healthy but unfortunately there are no guarantees.

How to choose your primary care physician

There has been a lot written about how to make the best choice of a primary care physician for you and your family. Some references suggest making an appointment and conducting a detailed and rather lengthy interview process with a potential physician. We do not believe that this is necessarily the best route to choose. Almost all physicians, even the good ones, will feel uncomfortable during this kind of interview. Don't forget that while you are interviewing the doctor, you are also being interviewed. Although an interview may address a predetermined list of issues it does not truly evaluate how your doctor will deal with you or your family when you are sick.

There is no substitute for the "word of mouth" method. Good recommendations from friends are the most valuable information that you can gather. We advise that you do a survey and ask as many people as possible about their experiences, good and bad. Once you have narrowed your choice to a few physicians (that are accessible to you if you belong to a group health provider) then call the office and ask a few quick and basic questions.

information

1) Is Doctor ____________ accepting new patients? (If you are new to the area, always mention this in your opening questions.)
2) What are the office hours?
3) Does he/she do obstetrics, pediatrics…? (If your family needs special services.)
4) If I called for an appointment today when would I be seen?
5) Does Doctor ____________ return patient calls or is there a designated nurse for advice?
6) What do we do if we need help outside of office hours?

These questions will give you an idea of how an office operates. You have to judge how it will suit your needs. Remember, if your friends say that Doctor _________ is a caring person who is willing to listen to them, he/she will likely treat you in the same way.

information

When you go to the doctor

How to prepare for a visit to the doctor

1 *Bring a problem list.* This is a good idea because it is often difficult to remember everything when you meet with your doctor. A thorough list also gives the doctor a more complete picture of your problems which can be useful as symptoms are often associated with one another. Try to limit your visit to two major concerns. Trying to do too much may be dangerous. This is even more important when medication changes result from the visit.

2 *List your problems in order of importance.* The doctor needs to know which problems are bothering you the most and which are only minor. If possible, he/she would like to deal with what is the most important to you.

3 *Be prepared for change.* It is very important that you realize that what you and the doctor see as the most important problem may be different. Your biggest problem may be a corn on the bottom of your foot that gives you pain with every step. You may be less concerned with the fact that you get a tight chest when you walk up a hill because you only do it once a week. The doctor may choose to ignore the sore foot in favor of the chest problem as he recognizes it as a possible sign of something more serious. He/she may bump it to the top of the list though you may have had it near the bottom.

4 *The symptom that never gets dealt with.* This is a common frustration that comes about because the physician always deals with something else and never gets around to that one nagging symptom. There is an easy way to solve this problem. You should book an appointment exclusively for this symptom. Don't try to squeeze it in when you are at the doctor's for another reason. Tell the doctor that there are no other complaints or symptoms that you need dealt with today. Just that one. This will usually get him/her to address that specific symptom to your satisfaction.

5 *Bring a list of all your medications.* It is vital that you tell your physician everything that you are taking. This includes all over-the-counter medications, vitamins, supplements, and "natural" remedies.

6 *Know your symptoms.* Your physician will be more likely to diagnose your problem correctly if you can give him/her good information. Be prepared to answer questions such as: When did the symptom start? What makes it worse? What makes it better? Have you had this before? Are there other associated symptoms? Have you tried any home treatment?

7 *Watch for a pattern.* This is the most important information you can bring to your doctor. What do the activities of daily life (exercise, rest, eating, sitting, having a bowel movement…) do to your symptom? If your symptoms are related to eating it is advisable to keep a food record and compare it to the timing of symptoms. Physicians may make a diagnosis based on the pattern of discomfort rather than the type of pain or discomfort described. Helping to establish a pattern of symptoms is an easy and yet vital way to be active in your health care.

What you should know when you leave the doctor's office

1) What the doctor feels the diagnosis is.
2) What you can do to help yourself.
3) If testing is to be done, how does the testing affect the treatment plan?
4) If there is a new medication; What is its name and dosage? Does it replace an existing medication? What is it supposed to do? What side effects should I look for and what should I do if they appear?

information

General information about medications, alternative therapy and immunization

Let's talk about medication side effects

Individuals may react differently to medications. Therefore when we take what is considered to be even the most common and safest of medications, the list of potential side effects is overwhelming. When you have a medication that has been used billions of times the possible side effects are going to be too extensive to list. If you ask a physician to give you a list of side effects for a medication, the list may scare you away from something that may be important for you to take. Many of the side effects are rare and thus highly unlikely to occur. We believe that it is important for patients to concentrate only on the serious side effects that should result in their seeking advice or stopping the medication. Ask your doctor if there are specific side effects that he/she believes you should look for.

Alternative medicine

In recent years we have seen a substantial increase in the use of various forms of alternative medicine. Perhaps the largest increase has been in the area of herbal medicine. It has become a multi-billion dollar industry.

If you ask your doctor about a certain herbal remedy it is difficult to predict what type of response you may get. Most physicians have not been trained in this field and will be hesitant to give you a definite answer. This is reasonable as it is undesirable for any professional to give advice about something that is outside their area of training. On the other hand some physicians, because of a personal interest in herbal or naturopathic medicine, may be very knowledgeable.

The most common objections to herbal medicine that a physician may have center around the following factors:

1) The products may not be properly regulated for purity and consistency of dosage.
2) Many products have not been subjected to proper scientific testing to ensure their safety and demonstrate that they are truly useful in specific conditions.
3) They are marketed as being more "natural" and therefore are safer products.

information

One of the reasons new medications are so expensive is that they are so closely regulated that it takes hundreds of millions of dollars to pass the necessary testing to get a new product to market. Herbal medications are marketed as "foods" or "dietary supplements" and are not to be prescribed for any specific illness. This allows the sale of products which may not have undergone adequate testing for safety, or effectiveness.

Don't be fooled by the term "natural." It is a sales term more than anything else. Just because things are natural doesn't mean they are good or healthy for us. Don't forget that tobacco, marijuana, and heroin are also "natural." Cocaine and heroin were "wonder herbs" of their day when they were first used. It would be foolish to believe that we have found all the "bad herbs." Some herbs readily available in stores today are known to be toxic to the heart, kidneys, and our nervous system. It is useful to note that many of the conventional medicines your doctor uses which come from herbs have been tested. The difference between herbs and medicines is a very artificial one and they should all be treated as medications. We are not telling you never to use them, we just want you to give them the respect they deserve.

Many doctors believe that some of these herbs could be useful, others may do nothing, and others yet may be harmful. What makes most physicians uncomfortable is that it is uncertain whether anyone knows for sure which category each herb falls into. Please advise your physician as to what you are taking. It is very important that he/she be aware of your current medications.

information

Immunizations

It was only a short time ago that diseases like polio, small pox and diphtheria ravaged our society and took many lives. Despite what you may read, immunizations have proven to be both safe and effective. Because of their effectiveness many people have either forgotten or have never realized just how serious these illnesses were. As a result they have lost their fear of them. When you have no fear of the disease, the minimal risks of immunization become easier to focus on. Don't be fooled: these diseases were not trivial. Immunization does not weaken your immune system. In fact, it stimulates our natural defense mechanisms to be in a ready state just as disease does. In this way we get the immune response without getting the disease itself.

The risks of disease far outweigh the risks of immunization

Please check with your doctor's office for a schedule of immunizations to see if you and your family are up to date.